THE
JOURNEY
HOME

Books by Phillip L. Berman

The Courage of Conviction (editor)
The Search for Meaning
The Courage to Grow Old (editor)
The Ageless Spirit (with Connie Goldman)

THE
JOURNEY
HOME

*What Near-Death Experiences
and Mysticism Teach Us
About the Gift of Life*

PHILLIP L. BERMAN

POCKET BOOKS
New York   London   Toronto   Sydney   Tokyo   Singapore

POCKET BOOKS, a division of Simon & Schuster Inc.
1230 Avenue of the Americas, New York, NY 10020

Berman, Phillip L.
    The journey home / by Phillip Berman.
        p.   cm.
    Includes bibliographical references.
    ISBN: 0-671-50245-X
    1. Near-death experiences. 2. Near-death experiences—Religious
aspects. I. Title.
BF1045.N4B47   1996
133.9—dc20   96-33698
                                                            CIP

First Pocket Books hardcover printing December 1996

10   9   8   7   6   5   4   3   2

In Loving Memory of
Channa Rose Berman
June 8, 1993

ABOUT THE STORIES

The bulk of the stories featured in this book represent material gathered during interviews conducted over the past eight years with a wide variety of Americans who underwent either near-death experiences or mystical experiences. Whenever possible, I have used the true names and identifying characteristics of those I interviewed. However, a few people requested that I alter their names and some of the details of their stories to protect their identity. This I have done.

Occasionally, I have quoted small selections from the stories of men and women I did not interview myself. I acknowledge the sources for these quotes in the notes collected at the back of this book. I also provide a detailed bibliography for those who wish to explore the subjects I touch upon in greater detail.

ACKNOWLEDGMENTS

While this book represents a personal statement based upon nineteen years of experience as a comparative religionist and oral historian, I am, nevertheless, deeply indebted to the writings of Martin Buber, Viktor Frankl, Albert Einstein, Albert Schweitzer, Abraham Maslow, William James, and Carl Jung. In the course of producing this book, I was frequently struck by the degree to which these visionary thinkers have shaped my convictions about the nature of spiritual life. I would also like to thank Raymond Moody, Kenneth Ring, Michael Sabom, Sogyal Rinpoche, and David Lorimer for their collective reflections on the nature of near-death experiences.

My hat must also be tipped to my able and industrious editor, Claire Zion, who brought me to Pocket Books. Working with her has been a delight. Thanks, too, must go to Paul M. Hancock for his enormous generosity to the Lifebridge Foundation, a nonprofit organization dedicated to promoting the concept of the interconnectedness of all life. With the gracious assistance of Larry Auld, the Lifebridge Foundation's program director, I was offered a generous grant to cover the cost of transcribing the many interviews that animate the pages of this book.

My agent, Jonathan Lazear, deserves special credit for his wisdom, and the abundance of his outrageous jokes. Thanks also to Rhea White, of the Academy of Religion and Psychical Research, and to Nancy Evans Bush, president of the International Association for Near Death Studies.

To my many friends at the Hospice of the Western Reserve, who have taught me so much about what it truly means to care for the dying, I can only ask you to take a bow. Bravo! My son, Aaron, must also be commended for allowing his dad to write undisturbed in the afternoons after preschool. And my ever-supportive wife, Anne, was kind enough to offer her magnificent editorial advice on numerous occasions.

Finally, not included in this book are the stories of approximately one hundred people I interviewed. To each of you I express my apologies and gratitude.

Contents

PART THREE

MIRRORS OF THE HEART: MYSTICISM AND THE NEAR-DEATH EXPERIENCE

THE
JOURNEY
HOME

INTRODUCTION
THE LESSON OF DEATH

∞

On June 8, 1993, at approximately 7:00 P.M., I stood in a tiny, white-walled, single-bed recovery room at the Boulder Community Hospital, in Boulder, Colorado, cradling in my arms the delicate, six-pound-nine-ounce body of my baby daughter, Channa Rose Berman. Channa means "grace" in Hebrew, and her birth was to be one of great celebration for my family. Yet the sad truth we faced was that Channa had died just a few hours earlier in the hospital's emergency room after a frenzied C-section delivery. My wife, Anne, had put up a valiant struggle, and the hospital's doctors and staff had done everything they could, but Channa could not be saved.

So there I stood by Anne's bedside with Channa's silent body in my arms, our faces sheathed with tears. Anne was still groggy from sedatives, barely able to open her eyes, and striving mightily, although unsuccessfully, to cope with this devastating loss. She was in shock, and I was too, but her need for my care made it impossible for me to fully let go into my grief. Yes, our daughter had died and I was saddled with horrible pain, but she needed me now more than ever. And our three-and-a-half-year-old son, Aaron, needed me too.

As anyone who has ever experienced a death in the family knows, when someone dies, the world does not automatically come to a stop. Unlike in plays or books, curtains don't fall and chapters don't close. Life flows on. I first learned this truth at the age of fourteen, in 1970, as I watched my stepmother slowly slip to the ravages of leukemia, and learned it yet again in 1974, when I lost my father to colon cancer shortly after my eighteenth birthday. When someone dies, you see, there is still 6:00 o'clock, 7:00 o'clock, 7:20, 7:21 . . . and you've got to do something with yourself. My most immediate concern in the wake of Channa's death was to comfort Anne. But after she drifted off to sleep with the help of sedatives, sometime around 8:30 P.M., my concern instantly shifted to Aaron. I had to get him some food, to help him come to grips with what had happened to his much-anticipated baby sister, and to see that he got some sleep.

Aaron and I arrived home from the hospital around 9:15 P.M., already a good hour past his bedtime. I made him a quick bowl of macaroni and cheese, set him up at the kitchen counter, and quietly slipped away to my bedroom to face my grief alone. It wasn't that I was afraid to let my son see me cry, only that I didn't want to add additional stress to what had already been a day of trauma for both of us. I was worried about what he would make of his sister's death and whether I would be up to the task of explaining it to him. Can a three-year-old really understand the meaning of death, I wondered? Can any of us?

Aaron managed to gobble up his food more quickly than I expected and snuck into our bedroom, where he found me sitting in bed quietly sobbing. With amazing calm and assurance, he scrambled onto the bed, put his arms around me, and asked if I was sad about Channa's death.

"Yes, I'm very sad, Aaron. Channa just wasn't strong enough to survive and she died."

"I'm sad, too, Dad," he quietly replied.

A few minutes went by as we sat together on the bed, holding one another. Then Aaron made it clear to me that he was just as busy trying to make sense of Channa's death as I, for he hit me with a question he had obviously been ruminating over.

"Where was I before I was born?" he asked.

Years before, the distinguished Unitarian minister Forester Church had told me this question was very much on the minds of young children. But when it came from my own son, it took me by surprise. Yet when I thought about it, it made perfect sense. Asking where you were before you were born is clearly a much more relevant question to a child than the question we adults so often ask: "Where will I go after I die?"

Without realizing it, Aaron managed to see that there is a mystery at the core of our births as well as our deaths and that the answer to one question is the answer to the other. Yes, "Where was I before I was born?" is much the same question as "Where will I go after I die?"

I was surprised at how quickly I was able to answer Aaron's question: "You came from a warm and loving home, son, and that is also where Channa is going." It occurred to me then that the passage into life is identical to the passage out—it is a journey home. In essence, this book is an exploration of the paradox at the heart of this truth.

There are times in life for all of us that are somehow revelatory, which serve to bring some of the hazy, shrouded truths of our lives into sharper focus. This was just such a moment for me, for amid the great agony I felt over losing Channa, I came to see that I possessed an enormous sense of belonging to the universe that amounted to a deep-seated faith in the unity of creation. I wasn't concocting a comforting fiction to make Aaron feel better, or to skirt the issue of death altogether; I was sharing with him what I believed in my heart to be true, and it took me by surprise because I had never consciously articulated such a faith before.

Faith has never come easy to me. I have always possessed

a fairly cautious, skeptical temperament, which I inherited from my scientifically minded father. A hard-nosed trial lawyer and avid reader of history, it was never enough for him to believe in something just because it made him feel good. It also had to be true; strictly verifiable according to the principles of the scientific method. Like so many of his generation, my father grew up believing wholeheartedly in E. I. Dupont Company's 1950s-era slogan "Better Living Through Chemistry." Through science, my father believed, we could bring about the kingdom of heaven on earth without any assistance from God. Why resort to the mysterious world of spirituality?

While my faith in the virtues of science has never been as strong as my father's (after all, along with our microwave ovens we also got the atom bomb), I have generally carried his skeptical outlook with me in my work as a writer, sociologist, and oral historian. This was especially the case in my work as director of the Center for the Study of Contemporary Belief, a small nonprofit academic research consortium I helped to found in 1982. Dedicated specifically to chronicling the rapidly changing landscape of American beliefs, the Center is perhaps best known for its highly praised anthology of the beliefs of prominent contemporaries, *The Courage of Conviction* (1986). Its eight-member advisory board is comprised of serious-minded scholars, each of whom is a member of the American Academy of Religion.

So how does a man like me achieve such a faith in the unity of creation and eternal life? This is a difficult question to answer in a single sentence, because my faith has grown gradually, as it does with most of us. While a few men and women I have met have been gifted with a single moment of profound illumination that forever transformed them (as so often happens with near-death experiencers), most of us tend to point to a variety of what I call "pivotal episodes of change." Such episodes can be triggered by a multiplicity

4

of circumstances, but they invariably serve to quicken our thoughts or arouse our feelings to such an extent that we are forced to reassess our fundamental beliefs—and therefore also our lives.

The pivotal episode that first encouraged me to consider the possibility of life after death occurred in the spring of 1972, when I nearly drowned while trapped underneath a capsized sailboat in Los Angeles Harbor. I was sixteen years old at the time, sailing alone on a small fourteen-foot catamaran in an area near San Pedro affectionately known to local sailors as "Hurricane Gulch." There certainly wasn't a hurricane in force that day, but the eighteen-knot breeze that was blowing was quite sufficient to submerge my leeward bow while racing downwind, which in turn flipped the little catamaran end over end, cartwheel style.

A small catamaran's flipping is not an uncommon occurrence on a windy day, and, generally speaking, these corky little boats are pretty easy to bring back up. The problem I faced was that as the boat went over, a hook on my trapeze harness (the vest I used to hang my body from a wire off the side of the boat while racing upwind) got caught in the lacing that strung together the boat's plastic, trampoline-style deck. When the boat finally came to rest, upside down, I was trapped below the surface. Each of the boat's fiberglass hulls were filled with air and foam flotation devices, which made it virtually unsinkable, but I could not pop my head up through the trampoline. The maddening thing was that I was so close to the surface—less than a foot away—that I could see bright rays of light streaming eerily in through the trampoline lacing.

After struggling to free myself for a minute or so, the sheer terror of the moment ripped at my soul with a vengeance and I began to panic. I remember thinking to myself, This just can't be. I'm less than a foot from air, yet I can't breath. I'm going to die! I soon lost consciousness and had what near-death researchers have come to call an out-of-body experience. I found myself hovering over the boat, looking down through the water and the lacing of the trampoline at my trapped body. I then remember seeing my life flash before me in what seemed an instant and crying out loud that I didn't want to die, was too young to die. Then I vaguely remember visualizing a copy of the *Newport Daily Pilot* (the newspaper I delivered as a boy) and reading a blazing front-page headline: "Newport Beach Attorney's Son Drowns in Los Angeles Harbor." That's the last thing I remembered, for I immediately came to, made one last mighty lunge upward, and managed to free myself from the trampoline.

When I finally emerged on the surface, clinging to one of the upside-down hulls, I felt as though I had taken a punch to the chest as I strained to fill my collapsed lungs. Within a short period of time my boat was towed to a nearby shore by the Los Angeles Harbor Patrol. A bystander immediately ran over to see if I was all right. He told me that he was sure I was going to drown, estimating I had been trapped underwater for about five minutes. Shaken and distressed by the experience, but fearful of what my parents or friends might say if I shared with them the details of this inscrutable encounter with death, I said nothing. And within a few shorts months I was able to put the trauma behind me. Yet a nagging question remained in the back of my mind: Did I really leave my body, or was I just hallucinating?

Six years later, in the fall of 1978, I got closer to an answer when I had a profound "peak experience" that irrevocably altered the course of my life. I was a student of social ecology at the time, working on an undergraduate degree at the University of California at Irvine. One sunny afternoon, while walking on a nearby beach, I stumbled across a whirling dust devil that hovered before me for what seemed a long period of time. As I stood there on the beach, I was instantly transfixed by the simple beauty and wonder of this miniature tornado dancing before me. It struck me then that this dust devil was a vanishing point of immeasurable beauty, never to appear in the same place or form for the remainder of eternity. As I gazed more deeply at the dust devil, I suddenly felt myself merge with it, and from there, with all of creation. And as anyone who has ever had such a peak experience will tell you, there are few words to describe the sense of peace and comfort that arise when one momentarily feels oneself absolutely and completely at home in the universe, so deeply connected with all of creation that time comes to a halt as the doors of eternity swing open, freeing one's mind entirely from any sense of fear and filling it with unimaginable elation.

The power of this pivotal episode immediately compelled me to look more deeply into the subject of peak experiences, leading me to the writings of psychologist Abraham Maslow, to William James's seminal study of mystical experiences, *The Varieties of Religious Experience*, and to Martin Buber's profound reflections on spiritual life in *I and Thou*. I rapidly came to see that I was not alone, that others had undergone similar experiences of a deep sense of connectedness with creation, and that something was decidedly missing from the materialistic perspective I was absorbing as a student of social ecology. Wanting to learn more, I immediately changed my major to philosophy and religion. I can remember telling my friends at the time, "I think I'd better learn how to live before I decide how to make a living."

Seven years later, after completing my graduate studies at Harvard in comparative religion, I set to work on an extensive oral history of American beliefs and values under the auspices of the Center for the Study of Contemporary Belief. This project, which eventually came to be called *The Search for Meaning*, officially commenced in the winter of 1986. Over the following three years it would take me to twenty-three different states, leading to over five hundred hour-long interviews with men and women from a rich diversity of backgrounds, including meetings with the Grand Wizard of the KKK, Benedictine monks, farmers, housewives, and Wall Street stock traders, among others.

After completing this extended exploration of the American moral imagination in 1989, I was struck by two significant findings that piqued my curiosity. One was that a few of the men and women I interviewed shared with me elaborate accounts of near-death experiences. These accidental encounters seemed to confirm the startling findings of a large 1981 Gallup poll that found that nearly eight million Americans (or one out of twenty at the time of the poll) had undergone NDEs. The second finding was that the stories of those who underwent NDEs were remarkably similar to the ones shared with me by those who had undergone mystical moments. These similarities included experiences of becoming one with an indescribable light, a deep sense of connectedness with the totality of creation, a strong sense of belonging and gratitude, and a renewed sense of meaning and purpose.

While there were a few important differences between the stories of those who had near-death experiences and those who had mystical experiences (which I will touch upon later in this book), there were many common elements. Even more striking was the fact that the spiritual perspective of nearly every person I interviewed who had undergone such experiences was greatly transformed. I promised myself at the time that I would look into the subject more deeply, but found myself happily occupied for the next several years with two projects on the spiritual dimensions of late life, *The Courage to Grow Old* (1989) and *The Ageless Spirit* (1993).

In the several months following my daughter's death, I finally set aside the time, no doubt by inner necessity, to immerse myself in the literature on NDEs. One thing that baffled me about the many books I read is that a significant number of them actually seek to prove the existence of life after death rather than explore the profound spiritual implications of these experiences. While I certainly understand how crucial it is for each of us to verify the truth of our convictions, it seems pretty obvious that scientific efforts to prove the existence of life after death (like those that seek to prove the existence of God) are slated for failure from the outset. In part, this is so simply for semantic reasons. After all, so long as death is arbitrarily defined, as it was recently in *Lancet,* the British medical journal, as "just beyond the point from which anyone can return to tell us anything," the testimonies of those who have had near-death experiences will do little to sway the opinions of committed skeptics. *Lancet's* definition of death is obviously as subjective and nonscientific a statement as any, yet it is clear that as long as we yield the privilege of defining life and death to materialistically minded scientists, there is no hope of proving (or disproving, for that matter) the existence of life after death to everyone's satisfaction. The vast majority of clinical near-death researchers all eventually and reluctantly admit this, despite their carefully controlled research. So the debate continues.

I saw no point in covering this same territory in yet another book. Were these people hallucinating? Did they really leave their bodies? Are NDEs the result of oxygen deprivation? Psychological stress? Or are they merely the wish-fulfilling dreams of troubled souls? These are undeniably interesting questions. We could keep ourselves occupied with them for hours on end, much as we could playing a game of chess. Yet as the philosopher Kierkegaard once reminded us, those who take spiritual life seriously eventually lose interest in "interesting questions," or "interesting people" for that matter. This may explain why the great saints and seers of human history were seldom drawn to

9

circular pursuits that only enabled them to "kill time." Instead, there was but one question that persistently cried out from their souls: How is meaning to be found? In other words, they wanted not only to live, but to live fully, vitally, and meaningfully—they desired to live spiritually.

Near-death experiences and mystical experiences have much to teach us about the meaning of life. I say this because I am convinced that such experiences are moments of profound spiritual illumination that provide us with glimpses of an answer, hints of an explanation not only of what our deaths will be like, but of what our lives should be like. This is why my aim in writing this book is not so much to prove the existence of life after death as it is to prove that death holds far less fear for those who have learned to live. As I hope to show, each of us has the capacity, on a daily basis, to expand the sense of deeper meaning without having to undergo an NDE. In fact, if we sharpen our spiritual sensitivities, I believe we can all come to see, taste, and smell the unity of life with such an intensity that our sense of belonging to the universe will dispel any fears we might have that our deaths are in any sense final. The ultimate proof of life after death is unlikely to arise in a laboratory— it must emerge from our own spiritual experiences.

Life would be empty for all of us without a plentitude of spiritual experiences. I say this because my brief sojourn on earth has taught me that each of us is born with a deep craving, a bottomless need, to reconnect ourselves to that which is greater than we are. I do not hesitate to add that I am happy to call this greater something God. However, whatever term you use to describe that Mysterious Wider Reality at the core of all life, all things, all creation, is fine with me. Brahma, Yahweh, Allah, Tao, the Divine Source— any of these will do. The root of the word *religion* means "to bind" or "to connect," and it is easy to see that all of us are engaged in this "effort of connecting" ourselves to this Wider Reality we in the West have come to call God. Yet whether we call ourselves a Jew, a Christian, a Buddhist, or an atheist, it is meaning we are after, and spiritual experiences of unity, belonging, and community alone are capable of delivering that to us.

The good news is that spiritual experiences are not restricted to levitating saints, enraptured mystics, or magical gurus, but open to us all, because we are each born with the capacity to experience a profound sense of connectedness to life. It is in these moments of connection that we feel meaning and "meet God." In fact, any experience that is filled with a rich sense of belonging, and with the joy that inevitably springs from it, can be classified as a spiritual experience. Kissing a child, lighting a candle in a church, embracing a spouse or lover, hiking in the woods, planting a tree, lending a caring ear to a lonely soul—these are all spiritual experiences. While they may vary in kind and intensity, such experiences all serve to reinforce the same underlying truth—the beauty, the connectedness, the sacredness of life.

Given my conviction that spiritual experiences are the bedrock of meaningful living, it should come as no surprise that I have chosen to devote a portion of this book to religious history and mythology. In particular, I will briefly explore religious approaches to death from ancient to modern times. Death, after all, is the primary subject of this book, but it is also very arguably the great hub around which all religions turn. A recognition of death's importance and meaning is an integral aspect of nearly every ancient culture. Strikingly enough, there is broad agreement among the ancients, Western and Eastern, that an awareness of death is a necessary precondition for the attainment of wisdom. Plato went so far as to say that philosophy is nothing more than the art of preparing for death.

One thing I hope these brief excursions into myth and history will show is that NDEs have been painstakingly recorded for centuries, and that the accounts left us by the ancients are quite similar to the many moving stories that were shared with me by contemporaries. In particular, the passage from darkness to light, from a sense of fear and estrangement to a sense of joy and homecoming, has been a universal theme in the world's religions since the beginning of recorded history. Why this is so is an important question, one that I will explore in the pages that follow.

Perhaps all that I hope to say about the subject of death and spiritual life in the pages that follow can be summed up in the seldom-used Hebrew expression, *neshameh yeterah,* which means "additional spirit," or "additional soul." In days gone by, the great rabbis used to say that the truly spiritual Jew was filled with *neshameh yeterah,* particularly on the Sabbath. And who among us would not wish to be filled with such additional soul? In Christianity, the saintly person is said to be filled with it, crowned with a halo of "pervasive luminosity and brilliance," as my wife once wrote. In Buddhism, the Boddhisatvas are said to be filled with it. In Hinduism, the swamis are said to be filled with it. Likewise, I believe, the men and women who have undergone NDEs have also been momentarily filled with *neshameh yeterah,* for like the great mystic seers down through the ages, they have been graced to enter into a powerful encounter with God. The good news, of course, is that all of us can be filled with such additional soul, so long as we are willing to devote ourselves to the task of becoming, as D. H. Lawrence once so tenderly put it, "a creature in the house of the God of life."

The eighth of June, 1993, will forever be etched in my soul as a pivotal episode of pain and spiritual illumination for me, for as I rocked my baby daughter slowly in the hospital maternity ward that day, I came to understand, perhaps for the first time in my life, what Albert Schweitzer meant when he spoke about "reverence for life," for death has a way of putting our miraculous lives into proper perspective. Now whenever I feel the tendency to complain or moan, I try to remind myself of the opportunity Channa was denied, for human life is a privilege denied to many. As I have come to see, it is often our simple failure to be ever mindful of this fact that so often strips the joy from our living—and from our dying as well.

Since my little daughter was not given the opportunity to imbibe the scent and splendor of this little blue jewel we call the earth, the best I can do is dedicate this book to her memory and to the task of rekindling our spirits so that we may live our lives as they were meant to be lived, with wholeness, caring, and love, and a great measure of awe and gratitude.

As Jesus reminded us, in the fullness of time we will all come to see that the secret to dying is to master the art of living.

PART ONE
WHISPERS
OF ETERNITY

1

RECOVERY
OF THE SOUL

∞

Do you see O my brothers and sisters?
It is not chaos or death—it is form, union, plan—it is eternal
life—it is happiness.
                                        —Walt Whitman, "Song of Myself"

What do you fear most about death?

Now there's a question that doesn't pop up too often at dinner parties or Sunday brunches. But it came up recently for me while participating in a hospice training seminar on the art of ministering to the dying. The seminar leader was teaching a segment on the necessity for "active listening," and one of the exercises she used to demonstrate the skill was to arrange her students in pairs so they might ask one another this troubling question.

My partner turned out to be an extremely intelligent social worker, a single mother with a cherished eleven-year-old daughter. She was also a woman greatly distressed by the prospect of death.

"What do you fear most about death?" I asked her.

"Oh my goodness," she replied. "There are so many things. First of all, I fear what is going to be on the other side—if there is another side. Am I just going to be some disembodied soul floating in ether? And what will happen to my daughter when I'm gone? What will it feel like to die? How can I look forward to death if I'm not sure it will be a good thing or a bad thing?"

Will my death be a good thing or a bad thing? For my partner, as for most of us, this is an undeniably troubling question. Yet for the hundred or so people I interviewed who had either undergone near-death experiences on the brink of death or who were once pronounced clinically dead in a hospital, it isn't a question at all. As near-death experiencer Lynn Pielage-Kissel, a woman from Dayton, Ohio, who nearly died in a skating accident, explained to me, "All through literature authors have written about the pain of death. But now I know that death isn't pain at all. . . . I know this to be true from my own NDE. . . . I know that the next time I die I will be shedding this human form to take on a new form of consciousness. I'm fully confident that another great adventure is sure to come."

Lynn's confidence in the reality of life after death is nearly universal among the more than eight million men and women who have had NDEs, which makes them extraordinarily unusual people. I say this because the many hundreds of Americans I have interviewed over the past decade generally told me they were immensely fearful of death. The novelist Philip Wylie addressed this truth when he noted that many conversations between doctors and their elderly patients often begin with "Doctor, lately I've been noticing . . ." To which Wylie jokingly added, "What they've been noticing is old George T. Death peering over their shoulders."

I was once taught that philosophy begins from the moment we start to question the truth of our parents' teachings. But now I see that it begins with this altogether natural, instinctual fear of "old George," for we all soon learn that here on earth, between time and eternity, the only certainty before us is an encounter with this shadowy stranger. What to make of this encounter, and just how to prepare for it, is a question on nearly everyone's mind.

Fear of death has been a universal ailment for millennia, of course. Modern people certainly don't hold a patent on it. Yet when I look around these days I see a culture that is utterly enchanted with youth and intensely fearful of old age, which leads me to believe that fear of death is extremely acute in our time, perhaps more so than in any period in history. There are surely many reasons for this, one among them being an advertising industry that relentlessly blitzes us with tantalizing images of the young and restless. But it really isn't fair to pin all of the blame on advertisers, because the primary sponsor of our fear is not a specific person or group. Rather, it is the widespread loss of spiritual vision evident in every sector of society. To paraphrase the Book of Proverbs: Where there is no spiritual vision, the people are likely to fear death.

The decline of spiritual vision in our time can be traced quite directly to the scientific revolution of the seventeenth century, which vigorously challenged the notion that an unseen spiritual plane could exist alongside the physical plane. Since that time, the entire trend in scientific research has been toward explaining all phenomena, including the human mind, as by-products of matter and physical forces. Everything can and must be understood and reduced to a physical cause. If it isn't physical—if it can't be measured, weighed, or seen, whether by telescope, microscope, or cyclotron—it does not exist. For those who view the world exclusively through such a lens, human consciousness is nothing more than a function of the physical brain: when the brain dies, we die. End of argument. Unfortunately, this limited view of life, death, and the nature of human consciousness continues to dominate the modern landscape for the very simple reason that science's many triumphs over the past 300 hundred years have been nothing short of dazzling. It is difficult to argue with success.

The Scottish philosopher David Hume once insightfully declared that "all advantages are attended with disadvantages." The advantages of the scientific outlook are pretty easy to spot. We enjoy them each day in our cars, refrigerators, computers, airplanes, and automatic coffeemakers. The disadvantages are more difficult to pinpoint because a few of the biggest ones are lodged quietly within the invisible domain of our minds. Perhaps the greatest of these is the harm this limited outlook has brought to the way we perceive the world. If there is one thing my travels throughout America have taught me, it is that millions of people today have nearly lost the capacity to experience a childlike sense of surprise and wonder in their lives.

A sense of surprise and wonder was hardly alien to the men and women who left us the sacred literature of the Bible, the Hindu Upanishads, or the Chinese Tao Te Ching. Unlike so many of us today, these premodern authors were not corrupted by the belief that everything could be measured, analyzed, and explained—and thus stripped of all mystery. A colorful sunset for them was a great deal more than the complex refraction of light across the stratosphere— it was a surprising gift of beauty freely given to them by God. Theirs was a world steeped with a sense of the miraculous. It was also a world filled with a perception of the divine, for they believed that something very mysterious and powerful must be offering up such enormous and surprising gifts—and they were deeply grateful to whomever (or whatever) this was. They saw the world through the wide eyes of a child, which explains why they all appeared to agree with Jesus that "Unless you change your life and become like a child, you cannot enter the kingdom of heaven." Unfortunately, such innocence does not come easy in our day. Yet once again, those who have undergone near-death experiences are an exception. Most of them return with reports not unlike that of Richard Alsop, a person from Los Angeles who has had a near-death experience:

> God didn't tell me how he made the world in my NDE. . . . All of the secrets to the universe were not revealed to me. But I did meet God in the light, and I did see that all of us are mysteriously connected to each other forever in a universe of such vast beauty that words cannot possibly describe it. . . . So now I see the world quite differently than I did before; everything has become more wonderful to me because now I know that everything is a gift from God—even my body.

The belief that life is a gift, a surprising and wonderful gift from the mystery at the heart of the universe, has been relentlessly challenged for the past three hundred years. A few great thinkers have valiantly sought to help us recover this missing sense of wonder and gratitude in our lives by pointing out the limits of science and the necessity for spiritual vision, among them William James, Carl Jung, Albert Einstein, and Viktor Frankl. But it has clearly been the aspiritual thinkers who have dominated scientific and academic circles for the past several decades. Jean-Paul Sartre, arguably the most influential philosopher of the twentieth century, was a militant atheist who said that the idea of God was impossible. Rather than God, he said, there was only nothingness, a nothingness that would inevitably engulf us at death, thus making most human strivings futile.

Although Sartre's dreary perspective is thankfully collapsing in the late twentieth century, giving way to a more balanced view of science and human spiritual aspirations, it continues to exert a powerful influence in shaping popular culture. Unfortunately, it has already done much to strip the soul out of life for many millions of people because it is exceedingly difficult to live vitally so long as we are convinced that all that we do, dare, dream, or scheme is ultimately fated to perish. How could one possibly feel at home in a universe where nothing mattered? Where nothing was wonderful? Nothing surprising? Nothing mysterious? Nothing truly awe-inspiring? Where could one find joy in a world such as this? Perhaps this is at least a partial explanation for why depression in America now outnumbers all other medical symptoms combined.

Given this deficit of spiritual vision, it is easy to appreciate why so many contemporary thinkers have arrived at the conclusion that what we suffer most from today is, as author Thomas Moore recently put it, "loss of soul." Surely the great task of the coming years is to recover that lost soul, to rekindle a sense of wonder and gratitude in our lives, to reclaim our sense of belonging to the universe—to feel, once again, that no matter where we are, we are always and forever home.

Fortunately, loss of soul is not a problem for everyone, least of all for the men and women whose near-death stories you are about to read. In fact, as you will quickly come to see, those who have undergone NDEs generally face an opposite problem: instead of being troubled by a loss of soul, they are emotionally and spiritually challenged by an excess of it, the overwhelming, overflowing sense of joy and gratitude they feel from living with the conviction that they belong to the universe—and always will.

While reading the stories in the following chapter, I encourage you to pay particular attention to the common themes that bind them together. While you will see that each of these stories is quite unique, you will also note they share a great deal. As I aim to show in the pages that follow, very similar themes have been a dominant feature in nearly every ancient mythology. They have also been reported by those who have had near-death experiences for centuries, long before the advent of contemporary near-death research. These same themes have also been reported by the thousands of men and women who have undergone profound mystical experiences throughout history, including Moses, Jesus, Buddha, Shankara, and Lao-tzu.

How, where, and why do these themes appear in the world's great religions and mythologies? Are these experiences actual encounters with God? Why do so many of the same themes appear in both NDEs and mystical experiences? What can these experiences teach us about religion, death, and the meaning of life? Is it possible for us to gain similar insights into the nature of death and spiritual life without having an NDE or becoming a professional mystic? These are just a few of the many questions I will explore in the pages that follow. But first, listen carefully to the stories of some of the men and women who have journeyed to "the other side" and returned to tell us what they saw.

2

A NEW SPIRIT OF BELONGING: TRUE STORIES OF NEAR-DEATH EXPERIENCES

∞

In His will is our peace; it is the sea into which all currents and all streams empty themselves, for all eternity.
—Dante

This unmistakable experience has been achieved by the mystics of every religion; and when we read their statements, we know that all are speaking of the same thing.
—Evelyn Underhill

And now faith, hope, and love abide, these three; and the greatest of these is love.
—Paul (1 Corinthians 13:13)

LOIS ERDMANN

Lois Erdmann is a housewife, a part-time secretary, and a member of the Good Shepard Lutheran Church in Bismark, North Dakota. Although for much of her fifty-six years she has been plagued by poor health, she's an amazingly attractive and radiant woman with a keen sense of humor. Her experience is an excellent example of what has come to be called the "classic near-death experience." She died in a hospital setting, left her body, encountered the light of

God and "felt at one with Him," traveled down a long dark tunnel,
and experienced a tremendous sense of emotional and spiritual eupho-
ria. She explains that she returned to her body so she could "help
my son Scott through the growth of his religious conviction"—a
purpose echoed by most of the mothers I interviewed who under-
went NDEs.

I grew up in a very conservative Lutheran family. And I've always attended church, and I've always believed in God. But it wasn't until I was forty, until I had my out-of-body mystical experiences, that I truly understood the meaning of my faith.

Although I had three beautiful babies born to me, I had numerous problems having children, including several miscarriages. After my last miscarriage I had a lot of medical problems and was in and out of the hospital a great deal of the time. So it was determined that after my fortieth birthday I would have surgery to stop me from having any more kids. The night before I was ready to go to the hospital, I went to bed with a euphoric feeling of anticipation. At first I just assumed it was because I figured I'm finally going to be well; I'm going to have energy and I'll be able to do all the things I want with my family. The next morning when I awoke, I still had this wonderful feeling. I really don't have words to describe it, but I awoke in the wee hours of the morning and realized I was going to die; that I would not survive the surgery. [She begins to cry softly.] And this made absolutely no sense to me; I mean, how could I feel so good knowing that I was about to die and knowing that I had three young children who needed me, a husband who needed my support, and a widowed mother who was very dependent upon me? It just made no sense to me that I should feel so good about dying. I knew that heaven was supposed to be a wonderful place, but I couldn't conceive of leaving my family. So I just kind of pushed it out of my mind.

Well, I checked into the hospital later that day, and the next morning I went into surgery. And something went wrong. I remember seeing doctors and nurses talking to each other, saying that something had gone sour and that without another surgery to check the internal bleeding—my lungs had collapsed—there was absolutely no hope. They kept trying to put the second surgery off, because they felt I was too weak, but then I guess the final hour came and it was either do it or don't do it. It was during that second surgery that I went into a coma for ten days.

During the coma I had my first out-of-body experience, which I remember vividly. This was when a young nurse came to check my vital signs and couldn't find any. And I remember observing this, watching her as if I were watching a movie of a nurse coming into a hospital and checking a patient's vital signs. I was looking down on the scene, like a spirit. As I was observing this young nurse, she panicked . . . so she kept taking my vital signs over and over again. I knew I couldn't communicate with her, but I wanted to reassure her that it was okay, that everything would be fine. Then she called for some assistance, and a team came in with the paddles to revive my heart. I remember them getting set up for that, but then I blanked out. . . .

The next experience, which followed very quickly upon that one, was my husband and my teenage daughter sitting at my bedside. I saw their positions, the clothing they had on, and I knew their thoughts. And their thoughts were that I was going to die. My daughter was wondering [she is weeping softly] how she was going to finish her life without her mother. She was a teenager, she had her whole life ahead of her, with dating, getting married someday, and all her thoughts were about how does one do this without a mother? How will I cope with these things without my mother? And yet she was not articulating these things in her own mind, but this was the emotion that was just charged through all her being. She was grieving for me, she was grieving for herself and her situation, and that's what was in her mind. My husband was experiencing somewhat the same thing, although he had a feeling of regret that he had not devoted more time to us, because he was so busy making a living for us, spending long hours at work. So he was feeling regret that he hadn't done more, and now it was too late. He was offering prayers—"God, if only it wouldn't be too late." But it was too late, and it was a conviction he had. So these were the emotions that were going on in them, and as I looked down on them, I wanted to communicate with them, I wanted to let them know that it was all right, that they should not have regret.

In my mind at the time was the phrase that Christ spoke to his disciples when they were in the boat during a storm. The disciples asked for help to get through, they wanted supernatural help to get through, and Christ said, "O ye of little faith." I had always read that as a rebuke, but then I saw that it wasn't a rebuke at all. It was Christ's expression of compassion and his understanding of their humanness: "If only you had more faith you wouldn't be experiencing all this fear and anguish." So when Christ said, "O ye of little faith," those were the words that came to me, and that's what I felt for my husband and daughter. I wanted them to have more faith, so they wouldn't be sad. And yet I understood and had compassion as to why they were experiencing this, because I understood then that the Christian promise was real. Christ was with me, God was with me, and there was nothing to be afraid of. In fact, were it not for the anxiety of my family, I would have felt wonderful, because I felt at peace not only with myself, but with my God. Anyway, I was very much aware of my family's humanity ... that this was the way it was. So I had a compassion; I really hurt for them, but there was a perfect peace within me; a peace like I'd never felt before . . . and I haven't experienced it since.

The next thing I remember was my son, Scott, arriving. I followed him walking down a lit corridor coming to my room. He did not like hospitals, and still does not like hospitals, but he knew that if he wanted to see me, he had to come. On the way to the hospital, he stopped in the produce department of a market and bought some flowers for me. And Scott is always the clown; when he's in an uncomfortable situation, he clowns. So he walked in the room talking about the flowers because he was very uncomfortable. He was chattering about the flowers, and then when he saw my lifeless body lying in that hospital bed he panicked and ran out of the room and down the corridor. A nurse saw him and asked if she could help him, and he thrust the flowers at the nurse and said, "Here, I brought these flowers for my mother, but I don't have a vase. Maybe you could get a vase and put them in water." Then the elevator arrived, he got on the elevator, and ran out of the hospital. And I remember thinking, if only Scott could understand. But I knew he would grow and understand some day, and I was only sad that he would have to learn that through a great deal of pain.

In her books, Elisabeth Kübler-Ross writes about others who have experienced life after death—but I didn't know about her work until a year after I got out of the hospital. She talks about the sensation of being in a tunnel, a very dark tunnel, and approaching light. And I felt that I entered and traveled down that tunnel, and it was the last and most powerful experience I had. It was interesting, because I had a feeling of peace and anticipation, but also a bit of discomfort, because there was this very uncomfortable sound. The closest thing I can relate it to is when my automatic washer is on spin—it was kind of that sort of hum. But the further I moved toward the light—the more I got inside the tunnel—the quieter the sound became. And I was glad to be leaving it behind. I did not see friends in the tunnel; I did not see people; and my life did not flash before me, which is different from some experiences I've heard of. All I remember is that I was getting closer and closer to the light. The light was pure and white, and yet it didn't blind me. It was not like trying to look at the sun on a beautiful hot day. It was comfort, and it was fine, and it was beautiful. I knew that the closer I came to the light, that at some point the light would envelope me and I would be on the other side. There was another side of that light, and I was sure of that, and I knew I was going to be there. I was anticipating it. It was warm, but there was no discomfort with it. And just as I was about to be enveloped—in a blinking of the eye I'd be across, and I could see that it was going to be perfection and wonder—I was sent back.

No words were spoken. I did not hear my Lord's voice, but I felt his presence and I felt at one with him. My sense of self slipped away and all that was left was inner peace. But I knew that I would be sent back, because I couldn't let go of my family. And I can't say that I regretted going back. Death was nothing to fear any longer, and I knew life wasn't permanent, so I came back without a regret. All I knew was that there was something left undone before I began my journey, so I had to come home and finish that. At the time, I believed that I was to come back and help my son Scott through the growth of his religious conviction, to explain to him death and dying and trust and faith. I knew I would do that, and I would be a part of Scott's Christian growth. It was a feeling of peace that, when the right time presented itself, words would flow. A greater power, which I believe is my Lord, or the Holy Spirit, would give me the words to say to Scott. There was no urgency to this, but I knew that I would not be returning until this was done.

That was sixteen years ago, and it wasn't until this past

Christmas that I became convinced that Scott had found his own deep Christian conviction. So maybe my mission is complete, but I can't be sure.

All I know from that experience is that I am here to glorify my Lord; the only reason I am here on earth is to glorify my Lord. I can do that in heaven, but the reason I'm here on earth is to allow myself to be used when he wants to use Lois. He uses many people to see that his will is done, that they live out their purpose in life. And each of us has a different way of fulfilling that potential. I believe that he wants me to live my life just as I am, adoring him, praising him, glorifying him, and then having that within me, that conviction in me, to reach out and touch others.

So now I'm doing all of the right things for the right reasons. When I was young, I did many good things, but they were done for the wrong reasons. Now I'm doing things to glorify my Lord, and [her voice is filled with warmth and excitement] it's a wonderful thing because before I do something now, I ask myself: Lois, why are you going to be involved in this? Is it to build your own popularity? Is that why you're doing it? Are you doing it for your own ego? Are you doing it because you want people to like you? Are you doing it because you don't want people not to like you? Why are you doing these things? If I become involved in this, is that going to glorify my Lord? Is it going to be using the gifts that he has given me in a very unique way? ... So you see, I believe that each individual on earth, no matter what your religious convictions are, is given gifts. And it's our choice whether or not we use them in a way that would give glory and honor to our Creator. How our Lord has honored me, and how he honors others, by giving us these opportunities—my God shares these things with me.

Dr. George Rodonaia

He holds an M.D., a Ph.D. in neuropathology, and a Ph.D. in the psychology of religion. Most recently he delivered a keynote address to the United Nations on the "The Emerging Global Spirituality." Before emigrating to the United States from the Soviet Union in 1989, he worked as a research psychiatrist at the University of Moscow.

I include Dr. Rodonaia's story here not only because it is dramatic and powerful, but because he underwent one of the most extended cases of a "clinical NDE" ever recorded. Pronounced dead immediately after he was hit by a car in Tbilisi, Soviet Georgia, in 1976, he was left for three days in a morgue. He did not "return to life" until a doctor began to make an incision in his abdomen as part of an autopsy.

Another notable feature of Dr. Rodonaia's NDE—and this one is common to many—is that he was radically transformed by it. Prior to his NDE he worked as a neuropathologist at the University of Moscow. He was also an avowed atheist. Yet after the experience, he devoted himself exclusively to the study of spirituality, taking a second doctorate in the psychology of religion. He then became an ordained priest in the Eastern Orthodox Church. Today he serves as an associate pastor at the First United Methodist Church in Nederland, Texas.

My mother was born in London. My father was born in Soviet Georgia. It would be a great understatement to say that my parents were not looked upon very kindly by the Communist government, because they believed strongly in human freedom and vigorously fought for it. They were courageous people, perhaps too courageous, because the KGB banished them to the *gulag* in the late 1940s for openly expressing their opposition to totalitarian government. So they spent many years in that horrid detention system made so famous by Alexander Solzhenitsyn in his masterful book, *The Gulag Archipelago.*

Sometime around 1948 my parents were ordered by the Soviet government to work on the Trans-Siberian Railroad. Many other dissidents were also forced to assist in this massive construction project. My parents worked on the railroad for about six years before I was born, in 1956, in Shanghai, China. Unfortunately, Khrushchev came to power shortly after that and operatives from his government charged my parents with spying. They were then murdered by the KGB. I was just seven months old.

I was then adopted by a family from Soviet Georgia. I was fortunate, because my adoptive parents showered me with love and wonderful care and took pains to educate me properly. They were not especially religious, not in an organized or outward way, but they were fantastic caring people. Unfortunately, my adopted father died of lung cancer when I was nine. Then my adopted mother died of pancreatic cancer when I was twelve.

At twelve I was living alone in the home left to me by my adoptive parents in Soviet Georgia. A few neighbors stepped in to feed me, to give me a hand, but I had to grow up quickly. I realized that the only way I would ever survive was to become strong and bright and able, so I applied myself to my studies very hard. I did a great deal of writing, too. I even wrote an essay which was published in the University of Moscow newspaper. The president of the university liked my essay very much; he liked it so much, in fact, that he invited me to attend the university at the age of fourteen. So I moved to Moscow.

At the University of Moscow I developed a great love for the physical sciences and medicine. My research specialty was concerned with adenosine triphosphate, or ATP, which is sort of an energizer for the brain. I was very much a typical young research scientist and a pretty skeptical one, too. I was not religious at all. I was an atheist. I had basically accepted the materialistic perspective of the hard sciences that everything can and should be reduced to a material cause. There was no room for spirituality for me at all; out of the question, totally out of the question.

Life became complicated for me at the age of eighteen, when I was invited to pursue advanced research at Yale University in 1974. The thought of studying at Yale and living in the United States thrilled me, but since I didn't have a wife or family members in the Soviet Union to discourage me from seeking asylum in the U.S., the KGB wouldn't let me go. By 1976, however, I was married and had a little son, so the Soviet government reluctantly agreed to allow me to go to the United States. Many people got involved to see that this occurred, among them Millicent Canter, a friend from Longview, Texas, who for many years sought to bring me to the United States. She even got Henry Kissinger involved in my cause, because he sent a letter on my behalf from the U.S. government to support my invitation. Unfortunately, as I would soon find out, the KGB had no intention of letting me go.

On the day of my scheduled departure for the United States, the KGB tried to kill me. I was waiting for a cab on a sidewalk in Tbilisi when I saw a car jump up on the sidewalk, avoid a few trees, and then head directly for me. It all happened in an instant. First I saw the car coming toward me, then I felt it hit me head-on. I estimate I flew about ten meters, landed facedown, and then the car ran over me again. From that time on, I must have been unconscious, because I can't remember anything else about the crash or the crash scene.

The first thing I remember about my NDE is that I discovered myself in a realm of total darkness. I had no physical pain, I was still somehow aware of my existence as George, and all about me there was darkness, utter and complete darkness—the greatest darkness ever, darker than any dark, blacker than any black. This was what surrounded me and pressed upon me. I was horrified. I wasn't prepared for this at all. I was shocked to find that I still existed, but I didn't know where I was. The one thought that kept rolling through my mind was, How can I be when I'm not? That is what troubled me.

Slowly I got a grip on myself and began to think about what had happened, what was going on. But nothing refreshing or relaxing came to me. Why am I in this darkness? What am I to do? Then I remembered Descartes's famous line: "I think, therefore I am." And that took a huge burden off me, for it was then I knew for certain I was still alive, although obviously in a very different dimension. Then I thought, If I am, why shouldn't I be positive? That is what came to me. I am George and I'm in darkness, but I know I am. I am what I am. I must not be negative.

Then I thought, How can I define what is positive in darkness? Well, positive is light. Then, suddenly, I was in light; bright white, shiny and strong; a very bright light. It was like the flash of a camera, but not flickering—that bright. Constant brightness. At first I found the brilliance of the light painful, I couldn't look directly at it. But little by little I began to relax. I began to feel warm, comforted, and everything suddenly seemed fine.

The next thing that happened was that I saw all these molecules flying around, atoms, protons, neutrons, just flying everywhere. On the one hand, it was totally chaotic, yet what brought me such great joy was that this chaos also had its own symmetry. This symmetry was beautiful and unified and whole, and it flooded me with tremendous joy. I saw the universal form of life and nature laid out before my eyes. It was at this point that any concern I had for my body just slipped away, because it was clear to me that I didn't need it anymore, that it was actually a limitation.

Everything in this experience merged together, so it is difficult for me to put an exact sequence to events. Time as I had known it came to a halt; past, present, and future were somehow fused together for me in the timeless unity of life.

At some point I underwent what has been called the life-review process, for I saw my life from beginning to end all at once. I participated in the real life dramas of my life, almost like a holographic image of my life going on before me—no sense of past, present, or future, just now and the reality of my life. It wasn't as though it started with birth and ran along to my life at the University of Moscow. It all appeared at once. There I was. This was my life. I didn't experience any sense of guilt or remorse for things I'd done. I didn't feel one way or another about my failures, faults, or achievements. All I felt was my life for what it is. And I was content with that. I accepted my life for what it is.

During this time the light just radiated a sense of peace and joy to me. It was very positive. I was so happy to be in the light. And I understood what the light meant. I learned that all the physical rules for human life were nothing when compared to this unitive reality. I also came to see that a black hole is only another part of that infinity which is light. I came to see that reality is everywhere. That it is not simply the earthly life but the infinite life. Everything is not only connected together, everything is also one. So I felt a wholeness with the light, a sense that all is right with me and the universe.

So there I was, flooded with all these good things and this wonderful experience, when someone begins to cut into my stomach. Can you imagine? What had happened was that I was taken to the morgue. I was pronounced dead and left there for three days. An investigation into the cause of my death was set up, so they sent someone out to do an autopsy on me. As they began to cut into my stomach, I felt as though some great power took hold of my neck and pushed me down. And it was so powerful that I opened my eyes and had this huge sense of pain. My body was cold and I began to shiver. They immediately stopped the autopsy and took me to the hospital, where I remained for the following nine months, most of which I spent under a respirator.

Slowly I regained my health. But I would never be the same again, because all I wanted to do for the rest of my life was study wisdom. This new interest led me to attend the University of Georgia, where I took my second Ph.D., in the psychology of religion. Then I became a priest in the Eastern Orthodox Church. Eventually, in 1989, we came to America, and I am now working as an associate pastor at the First United Methodist Church in Nederland, Texas.

Many people have asked me what I believe in, how my NDE changed my life. All I can say is that I now believe in the God of the universe. Unlike many other people, however, I have never called God the light, because God is beyond our comprehension. God, I believe, is even more than the light, because God is also darkness. God is everything that exists, everything—and that is beyond our ability to comprehend at all. So I don't believe in the God of the Jews, or the Christians, or the Hindus, or in any one religion's idea of what God is or is not. It is all the same God, and that God showed me that the universe in which we live is a beautiful and marvelous mystery that is connected together forever and for always.

Anyone who has had such an experience of God, who has felt such a profound sense of connection with reality, knows that there is only one truly significant work to do in life, and that is love; to love nature, to love people, to love animals, to love creation itself, just because it is. To serve God's creation with a warm and loving hand of generosity and compassion—that is the only meaningful existence.

Many people turn to those who have had near-death experiences because they sense we have the answers. But I know this is not true, at least not entirely. None of us will fully fathom the great truths of life until we finally unite with eternity at death. But occasionally we get glimpses of the answer here on earth, and that alone is enough for me. I love to ask questions and to seek answers, but I know in the end I must live the questions and the answers. But that is okay, isn't it? So long as we love, love with all our heart and passion, it doesn't matter, does it? Perhaps the best way for me to convey what I am trying to say is to share with you something the poet Rilke once wrote in a letter to a friend. I saw this letter, the original handwritten letter, in the library at Dresden University in Germany. [He quotes from memory, as follows:]

"Be patient with all that is unresolved in your heart. And try to love the questions themselves. Do not seek for the answers that cannot be given. For you wouldn't be able to live with them. And the point is to live everything, live the questions now, and perhaps without knowing it, you will live along some day into the answers."

I place my faith in that. Live the questions, and the universe will open up its eyes to you.

LYNN PIELAGE-KISSEL

She's a middle-aged corporate computer trainer and technical-support representative who makes her home in Fairborn, Ohio, a suburb of Dayton. She is also a practicing Buddhist who spends much of her free time in meditation.

I include Lynn's story here because she captures so well the profound experience of unity, belonging, and wholeness described by

37

the majority of near-death experiencers with whom I spoke. Her experience also led her to adopt a universalistic, nonsectarian spirituality, and convinced her of the "reality of reincarnation." And, like most near-death experiencers, she is certain that death is nothing more than a transition from one form of consciousness to another.

On June 21st, 1976, I was in a roller-skating rink, and we were dance-skating at a high rate of speed. I don't know how it happened, but I lost my balance and my skate wheels somehow got locked up with my partner's. In that instant, I went over sideways and then slammed head-first directly into the cement wall that circled the skating rink. I hit the wall with a terrible impact, bounced off of it, and then landed on the floor. My partner fell on top of me. When I opened my eyes, I was lying facedown in a rapidly expanding pool of blood. I knew I was in a lot of trouble. I remember I had this silly thought at the time that if I could just keep my eyes open I wouldn't die.

But as hard as I tried, I could not keep my eyes open. I knew I was about to die. When my eyelids finally closed, my vision exploded to such great dimensions that I thought I could see the whole world. I mean the sights and the sounds and the colors were so unusual that it was clear to me that something extraordinary was happening. I also remember that I became very aware of where I was inside my body, the fact that I was actually in it. Then I felt my heart's last beat, and when I exhaled for the last time, I felt relaxed and at peace. I even remember clearly that a smile came to my mind. This is great, I thought, now I don't have to breathe anymore. I never realized until that moment just how heavy my chest was and how much effort it took to inhale and exhale.

Almost instantly, I felt as though I was being pulled away from a shell; I felt my consciousness begin to separate from my body. I remember feeling my body temperature begin to drop rapidly, yet for some reason I felt like a very warm liquid inside this cool vial. Then, like a cork pulled out of a bottle, I just ran out of my body like liquid. Once I got out, I wasn't liquid anymore. I was more of just this form of indescribable consciousness. The best I can come to describe this is to say that I became a gaseous cloud of pure consciousness. Feelings of tremendous expansion and exhilaration beyond description rushed through me like a soft, warm breeze.

A short time after leaving my body I remember seeing myself lying on the floor of the skating rink on top of this large pool of blood. But it didn't scare me at all. In fact, I was overwhelmed with total joy, happiness, contentment, and a thousand more [feelings for which my words are] equally inadequate. My body was slow and heavy, and I was glad to get rid of it. It was confining, and I knew then how much it limited the range of my hearing and vision. Instead of information and stimulus slowly filtering into the brain through the senses, I could now absorb almost everything instantaneously, directly from the source. I felt swept up in a spectacular world of unlimited dazzling colors and magnificent sounds. These sounds were unlike any I had ever heard through human ears. High-pitched tones in rhythms, not in melodies, not like tinkling bells or anything like that. Just a pleasant blending of vibrations in harmony with thought.

When I looked down at my lifeless body, still facedown on the floor, I felt no remorse. The people hovering around me looked like a still-life painting. Their movements were barely perceptible from my position high above them. All I could think at the time was, I'm out! I am free for the first time! I mean I was elated. The dictionary has forty-one definitions for the word *free*, but none of them come close to describing the jubilation I felt from being out of this tiny container we call the human body.

I don't remember that anyone spoke to me, and yet I knew I wasn't alone. I felt no feeling of separateness, but rather this great feeling of being part of the whole. I remember, too, that I thought a great deal about my life, and that I judged myself to some extent, but my memories of this are vague.

Some people speak about seeing a bright light in near-death experiences, but I can't tell you that I saw such a light. What I saw was actually a lot of things, all against the backdrop of this field of gray that was getting brighter and brighter and brighter. Far off in the distance I remember a light, but it never dominated my experience as it appears to do for many other people. It was all lovely, and I wanted to see everything, hear everything, touch everything. I wanted to drink it in as fast as I could. A new beginning was unfolding before me. It seemed as though everything in the universe was right there before me and I was no longer hindered in any way from experiencing it all first-hand, without a single limitation. I felt this profound sense of knowing, and I wanted very much to just continue on in this expansion of consciousness. I felt so good.

I can't say how long all this took place, because time was nonexistent. All of this could have occurred in the blink of an eye or in minutes. But I do feel very certain that I could have stayed in this realm were it not for the fact that for a brief moment I thought of my two young daughters I was leaving behind. Almost instantly with this thought, a vacuum formed around me and I was sucked back into my body as though I had been shot from a cannon. Then the next thing I knew I opened my eyes and was back in my body. I was no longer on the rink floor, but somewhere in the common area of the skating complex. I felt this tremendous amount of pain, and I was having difficulty breathing. People were hovering all over me, and I could see the fear in their faces. I was then taken to the hospital, where I spent several weeks in recovery.

When I tell this story, most people normally say, "Oh, sure! You were probably just dreaming. How do you know you were really dead?" But I know I had the privilege of feeling my last heartbeat and experiencing my last breath in a state of complete awareness. I know I left my body, there is no question about this in my mind at all.

This experience really shook me up, because I had been brought up a Catholic, and I never even considered another belief system. But I discovered from this experience that much of what I had been taught in church was quite wrong. Death, from a Catholic's point of view, is that you either go to heaven or you go to hell. It is rather cut and dried. There is no gray area. And Catholics don't believe in reincarnation. But as a result of my experience, I became convinced in the reality of reincarnation. So I started reading about the subject and spent many months randomly and haphazardly studying the world's religions. I finally came to conclude that there was no one true religion, but found that of all the religions I came across, Buddhism made the most sense to me. So I converted to Buddhism about eight years after my NDE. I joined a group called Nicheren Shoshu, which is a widely practiced form of Japanese Buddhism.

This may surprise you, but twelve years after my NDE, on the same day, June 21st, I was in a terrible auto accident on Interstate 65, outside of Dayton. I flipped my car and it turned upside down on the freeway, and I was trapped for about an hour. I remember I could overhear the firemen and the paramedics outside saying they didn't think they could get me out without killing me. I wasn't sure if I was going to get out either, because I was hurt pretty badly. So I sat there and said to myself, Lynn, you've been here before, you've been dead before, so what are you going to do differently today than you did twelve years ago? I sat there and

I thought to myself, Is this a good day to die? And I said, Well, it is pretty much as good as any. My children are now grown up, so I don't have this tie anymore. So I thought, Well, if this is my time to die, I'm to die. So I sat and I chanted for a while. I was chanting, and I could see these firemen and paramedics outside desperately working to get me out of the car. I could feel their tension and anguish, but I felt perfectly peaceful and content. By this time they had flown in a helicopter to airlift me to the hospital. Finally, they cut the seat belt off and cut away the wheel and pulled me out sideways. I had no fear at all. I wasn't afraid. If this is my time, I figured, why not die with dignity. That's why my daughters have very explicit instructions never to allow me to be kept alive with life-support systems. When I'm to die, I want to die right then and there.

All through literature authors have written about the pain of death. But now I know that death isn't pain at all. As it is said in the Tibetan Book of the Dead, if there is any pain in death, it comes from fear: a fear of the unknown, a lack of being prepared to die. I know this to be true from my own experiences. If the body is in pain, it comes from clinging to life, from tightly grasping something that is slipping away. If we are able to simply let go of our bodies there is no pain whatsoever. Some people say that it is the consciousness holding on to the body that produces the fear, but I think it is the other way around: it is the body holding on to the consciousness that creates the pain.

For me, the veil between life and death is very sheer now. The space between the material plane and the spiritual plane is merely a thin pane of glass. Now I live with very little attachment to the earth, which doesn't mean that I don't like it, but that I know someday I will be leaving it behind. The only thing you can take with you when you die is the contents of your consciousness, because earthly attachments and material things are worthless. Now I know that the next time I die I will be shedding this human form to take on a new form of consciousness. I'm fully confident that another great adventure is sure to come.

DR. YVONNE KASON

She is a physician who practices family medicine and psychotherapy in Toronto, Canada. She is also an assistant professor at the University of Toronto and the author of three books, among them A Farther Shore, *which is about her NDE and her clinical work with hundreds of people who have had spiritual experiences. She is forty-two years old and the mother of a seven-year-old son.*

Dr. Kason's story is especially intriguing because she did not undergo a "classic NDE," but nevertheless experienced many of the same things we commonly associate with NDEs, among them an out-of-body awareness, a "blissful presence of God," and an immersion in "unconditional love." For many years she struggled to define her experience. Was it an NDE? Or was it a mystical experience? In her view, the distinction is now utterly irrelevant. What is important, she insists, is that "this experience made me a spiritual woman, because I now know to the core of my being, as a soul truth, that our spirits, or souls, live on after death."

My NDE occurred in 1979, when I was in a plane crash. I was a young medical doctor at the time, finishing up my specialty training. Part of this training required me to fly in small prop planes up into the remote northern regions of Ontario, Canada, to serve the medical needs of the native Indian communities. On one of these missions I had to accompany a critically ill Indian woman on a medical evacuation by airplane to a larger hospital because her condition was so critical that we couldn't deal with it in the small community hospital where I was working.

Anyway, the twin-propeller Aztec airplane we were flying in ran into a blizzard, and the air filters for the engines froze over. Each of the engines shut down, one after the other, and the plane went down. We crashed onto the surface of a semifrozen lake in a spot called, of all things, "Devil's Gap." When we hit the ice, the plane broke through and instantly began to fill with water. The pilot got out of the side door, pulling the plane's radio microphone and cord with him. He then immediately began to send out a Mayday call. My Indian patient was strapped to a stretcher on the floor of the plane. She was in a semiconscious state because she was heavily drugged. Within just a few seconds there was a two- or three-inch layer of water on the floor of the plane, so the nurse and I tried to float the stretcher over to the side door. Then the nose of the plane went down and water just began to rush into the plane in a torrent. The pilot screamed to the nurse and me to get out of the plane, so we made one last mighty effort to push the stretcher out the door, but we couldn't. The plane just sank, and along with it my patient.

The pilot yelled at us to try and get up onto a patch of nearby ice, so we all tried to do this. But the ice was too thin; each time we tried to climb up, the ice broke off in small chunks. Eventually the nurse managed to find a piece of ice with wood branches frozen into it, which made it float quite high. So she hung onto that. But the pilot and I had to swim about two hundred yards to shore in subzero weather, wearing heavy winter clothing. About twenty minutes later we were heroically, miraculously, rescued and taken to a nearby hospital.

The long and the short of it is that in the process of nearly freezing to death, and also nearly drowning, I had both a mystical and out-of-body experience, which I now believe was an NDE. The thing about my experience that was unusual is that it began before we actually crashed into the lake. It started when the two propellers stopped and I realized I was about to die. What happened was, I went, "Oh, God, I'm going to die." Just this wave of panic. And as my thoughts turned to God, it felt as if something was being poured into my consciousness—the Holy Spirit, if you like—and I started hearing words from the Bible. "Be still and know that I am God," was one of the most powerful phrases that was pouring into my consciousness. "God is with me now and always. God is my refuge and my strength." These verses were just flowing through my head. And with them came this incredible feeling of peace and calm and the presence of God.

When the plane actually crashed through the ice and began to sink, I was still in this state of peace and mystical calm. It was just this blissful presence of God. Then, as I was swimming to shore, I just lifted above my body, taking me about fifteen to twenty feet up in the air, so that I could look down on it all. I actually watched myself struggling to swim ashore. At the same time, I also felt surrounded by light. I went into a place filled with light. I felt immersed in unconditional love. I felt peace. I felt the presence of what I call God. I knew that I was dying, and yet I felt totally unafraid. I knew there was nothing to fear in death. Fear was totally incompatible with the state I was in.

When I was finally rewarmed in the hospital, my consciousness reentered my body. It felt like a genie being sucked into the bottle. Suddenly I was back in my body and I knew I was going to live.

This all occurred to me back in 1979, when very little was known about NDEs. So I spoke with my medical colleagues, telling them about this amazing thing that had happened to me. And everybody would put this medical label on it. "Well, you had hypoglycemia." Or, "It was just an electrolyte imbalance." Someone else said it was the "direct effect of hypothermia on the brain." These were all the interpretations people put on my experience. But the only person who said anything that resonated for me was a fellow who was a very devout Christian. He said, "Yvonne, you have had a mystical experience."

Did I have a mystical experience or a near-death experience? For eleven years I researched the subject of mystical experiences and NDEs. For most of that time I labeled what happened to me a mystical experience. I figured it couldn't have been an NDE because I was never really dead. I was fully conscious during the entire ordeal—or at least I felt I was. Still, I was troubled by the fact that I experienced most of the same symptoms as people who had described near-death experiences. I went out of the body. I saw a great light. I felt the presence of God. I felt warm. I felt loved. I experienced a profound sense of joy. And the fear of death left me entirely. So what does all this mean? My experience didn't fit the model of the classic NDE. Today, however, I believe I did have a mystical NDE that was brought about by my psychologically confronting death and turning to God for help.

This experience, of course, had a very profound effect upon me. It shifted my worldview and it continues to do so. The effects of this brush with death have been continuous. One of the major aftereffects it has had on me is in the way I deal with my patients, because I am open to listening to what they have to say, no matter how outrageous it may seem to other people. Another effect is that I have actively tried to raise awareness in the medical community about the undeniable existence of such experiences, and the power they unlock in people's lives.

Most profoundly this experience made me a spiritual woman, because I now know to the core of my being, as a soul truth, that our spirits, or souls, live on after death. I also know that there is a higher, loving, omnipotent, all-knowing intelligence that governs the universe. I am also convinced that every living human being—each of us—has a direct connection to this divine source, that we are all children of the same loving power, no matter what name we call it, if anything; God, Yahweh, the Tao, whatever you want to call it. There is but one source, and we are all directly connected to that source. So now I believe that our purpose here on earth is to grow as spirits, to learn to evolve. The bottom line is that what it is all about is love—loving ourselves, loving each other, loving the Divine. There is no greater truth, no greater aspiration than this.

3

FALLING INTO HEAVEN:
A BRIEF HISTORY OF
NEAR-DEATH RESEARCH

∞

The sheer volume of evidence for survival after death is so
immense that to ignore it is like standing at the foot of Mount
Everest and insisting that you cannot see the mountain.
—Colin Wilson

If life, or consciousness, failed to survive death, there would
be neither any meaning to life nor any ultimate justice. Nevertheless, many people believe that life does not continue after
death. Yet, as we often discover in life, what we believe may
have little or nothing to do with reality.
—Sogyal Rinpoche

The men and women who shared their stories in the previous chapter are amazing people. Not because they are especially wealthy, famous, or exceptionally gifted, but because
they died—or nearly died—and were fortunate enough to
come back to tell us what they saw. As near-death survivor
Phyllis Atwater nicely phrased it, "I am one of those people
who died but didn't stay dead . . . I passed through death."
These "lucky ones," like Atwater, have been much talked

about in recent years, because their claims radically contradict modern medicine's assumption that at death our consciousness will be extinguished like a flame. Their stories of life after death are so compelling, their experiences and insights so extraordinary, that they have spawned a wide array of books, articles, and television programs on NDEs over the past two decades.

I must confess that when I first encountered NDE stories in the late 1970s I didn't quite know what to make of them. While I had undergone an out-of-body experience of my own, as well as a powerful mystical moment of oneness, the elaborate stories of near-death experiencers initially struck me as a bit too far-out to take very seriously. Were it not for a chance meeting with Lois Erdmann, whose story appeared in the previous chapter, my opinion may never have changed. As she warmly and sincerely shared her NDE with me in Bismark, North Dakota, in August of 1987, any skepticism I might have had quickly vanished. While I was not certain that Lois had actually died and returned to life, I saw no reason to doubt that she had undergone a powerful experience on the threshold of death that changed her outlook on life forever.

I remember that after completing my interview with Lois I drove to a coffee shop to log her tape and reflect upon the meaning of her story. A sea of questions gathered in my mind: How frequent are these sorts of experiences? What sorts of people have them? What triggers them? What are the common elements, if any, that link them together? What are the spiritual implications for those who believe they have had such firsthand encounters with their God? And, most intriguingly, why were there so many striking parallels between Lois's NDE, my own peak experience, and the stories of the many mystical experiencers I had interviewed? When I finally set aside time to address these questions carefully, I decided to begin by acquainting myself with the short history of pre-death visions and near-death research. What do dying men and women see? And how do their brushes with death alter their understanding of life? In the previous chapter, the experiencers themselves told us what they believe. Here is what the researchers have had to say.

When most of us think about NDEs, the person who generally comes to mind is Dr. Raymond Moody, because he not only coined the term, *near-death experience*, but authored the first worldwide best-seller on the subject, *Life after Life*. Yet Dr. Moody is the first to admit that he is actually a member of a whole school of near-death (or pre-death) researchers, most of whom trace their roots back to the pioneering turn-of-the-century research of the Swiss geologist Albert Heim. An avid mountain climber, Heim was once hit by a gust of wind while climbing in the Alps and knocked off a rocky crag. Although his near-fatal fall lasted but a few seconds, something quite extraordinary happened to him on the way down.

I saw my whole past take place in many images, as though on a stage at some distance from me. I saw myself as the chief character in the performance. Everything was transfigured as though by a heavenly light and everything was beautiful without grief or anxiety, and without pain. The memory of very tragic experiences I had had was clear but not saddening. I felt no conflict or strife: conflict had been transmuted into love. Elevated and harmonious thoughts dominated and united the individual images, and like magnificent music a divine calm swept through my soul.

Although he did not undergo what is now called a "clinical NDE," the powerful emotional tone of Heim's story is obviously quite similar to the near-death accounts we just read, especially to that of Dr. Yvonne Kason. Heim under-

went a life-review process, felt surrounded by an atmosphere of tremendous love, and experienced a sense of unity,
beauty, and calm. This experience also proved to be transformative for Heim, because it compelled him to conduct a
number of studies with men and women who had undergone
a wide range of similar life-threatening situations, among them
soldiers wounded in battle, roofers who had fallen off buildings, and fishermen who had nearly drowned.

Heim's most important findings, however, were drawn
from his many interviews with fellow mountain climbers
who survived near-fatal falls. In a study he published on
the subject in 1892, Heim sought to show that death by
falling is actually a far more painful experience for onlookers
and relatives than it is for the victims themselves. He arrived
at this conclusion because 95 percent of the thirty fall survivors he interviewed told him they felt calm and joyful during their falls. As he wrote, "They had, so to speak, fallen
into heaven." He also noted that there was a stagelike progression to these experiences, beginning with enhanced and
accelerated mental activity, an unusually clear perception of
the outcome, an expanded sense of time, and a sudden,
rapid-fire life review. The culminating experience was a
powerful moment of joy and supernatural beauty, occasionally accompanied by the sound of peaceful music. Heim's
summary of the reactions of the mountain climbers is strikingly similar to the accounts of many near-death survivors:

> No grief was felt, nor was there paralyzing fright of the
> sort that can happen in instances of lesser danger....
> There was no anxiety, no trace of despair, nor pain; but
> rather seriousness, profound acceptance, and a dominant
> mental quickness and sense of surety.

Heim's research served as a tremendous catalyst for research on the visions of the dying, for within a few years

of its publication, numerous researchers picked up where he left off. The first among them was the British author F.W.H. Myers, who in 1903, produced a massive, two-volume study of deathbed visions, entitled *Human Personality and Its Survival of Bodily Death*. Four years later, in 1907, James H. Hyslop produced an influential article on the "Visions of the Dying" in the first issue of the journal of the American Society for Psychical Research. And then, in 1926, near-death studies received a tremendous boost when the prominent British physicist, Sir William Barrett, published *Deathbed Visions*, a full-scale study of the visions of patients in their final moments before death. Each of these studies confirmed Heim's initial insight that "The process of dying is far more frightening to onlookers than it is for the dying themselves."

Since 1959, Karlis Osis, of the American Society for Psychical Research, has carried on in Heim's footsteps. For the past thirty years he has been conducting a massive, ongoing study of the process of dying by analyzing the results of hundreds of questionnaires returned to him by doctors and nurses who have detailed the experiences of their dying patients. In 1972, with the help of Icelandic psychologist Erlendur Haraldsson, Osis extended his study to India in an effort to analyze the patterns of dying patients that cut across the boundaries of race and culture.

According to Osis and Haraldsson's research, among the 10 percent of patients who are conscious in the hour before death, a few experience vivid visions, often entailing graphic descriptions of the world to come, visitations from deceased relatives, encounters with a great light, and a profound sense of serenity. Far less common were reports of frightening, hellish visions. Osis summarized the results of his research as follows:

> Although most patients apparently drift into oblivion without awareness of it, there are some, clearly conscious

to the end, who say they "see" into the beyond and who are able to report their experiences before expiring. They see apparitions of deceased relatives and friends. They see religious and mythological figures. They see nonearthly environments characterized by light, beauty, and intense color. These experiences are transformative. They bring with them serenity, peace, elation, and religious emotions. The patients die a "good death" in strange contrast to the usual gloom and misery commonly expected before expiration.

Osis and Haraldsson eventually came to the conclusion that the many pre-death visions they studied were nearly identical to NDEs. The only notable difference they found was that pre-death visions occurred while a person was still conscious, whereas NDEs occurred while a person was "unconscious."

It was Dr. Elisabeth Kübler-Ross who first isolated the five stages normally experienced by those facing death—denial, anger, bargaining, depression, and acceptance. But the acknowledged expert on the psychiatric implications of both pre-death and near-death experiences is Dr. Russell Noyes, Jr., a professor of psychiatry at the University of Iowa, who first began publishing on the subject in the early 1970s. Together with his colleague, Dr. Roy Kletti, a clinical psychologist, Noyes has studied a significant number of personal accounts of individuals facing death. Noyes and Kletti also studied the autobiographical testimonies of exceptional individuals who had undergone peak or mystical experiences, among them the esteemed Swiss psychologist Carl Gustav Jung. As a result of a heart attack in 1944, Jung had a number of near-death visions that altered his entire understanding of human consciousness, which eventually compelled him to write that "What happens after death is so unspeakably glorious that our imaginations and our feelings do not suffice to form even an approximate conception of it."

After years of exhaustive research, Noyes and Kletti came to isolate several recurring patterns in the stories of the dying men and women they studied. They also identified three successive stages in the process of facing death. They called the first stage a period of "resistance," in which the individual first recognizes danger, fears for his life, struggles to save it, and then rapidly comes to accept death. In the second stage, people undergo a process of "life review," in which they experience a rapid, panoramic replay of the important events in their lives. In the third, and final, stage, the dying experience a sense of "transcendence," a mystical or spiritual state of mind in which they come to feel themselves a part of a larger reality, at which point the fear of death vanishes altogether. To illustrate these stages, Noyes resorts to the following story, splendidly told by an especially articulate woman who survived a dramatic crash after losing control of her car on a wet highway.

During the several seconds that my car was in motion, I had an experience that seemed to span centuries. I rapidly moved from sheer terror and overwhelming fear for my life to a profound knowledge that I would die. Ironically, with that knowledge came the deepest sense of peace and serenity that I have ever encountered. It was as though I had moved from the periphery of my being—the body that contained me—to the very center of myself, a place that was imperturbable, totally quiet and at rest. . . . Time seemed to have disappeared as I watched sequences from my life passing before me like a movie, quite rapidly, but with amazing detail. When I reached the point of death, it seemed that I was facing an opaque curtain of some kind. The momentum of the experience carried me, still completely calm, through the curtain and I realized that it had not been a point of termination, but rather of transition. The only way that I can describe the next sensation is to say that every part of me, whatever I was at that moment, felt without question a far-reaching and encompassing continuum beyond what I had previously thought of as death. It was as though the force that had moved me toward death and then past it would endlessly continue to carry through me, through ever-expanding vistas.

It was at this point that my car hit a truck with a great impact. As it came to rest, I looked around and realized by some miracle I was still alive. And then, an amazing thing happened. As I sat in the midst of the tangled metal, I felt my individual boundaries begin to melt. I started to merge with everything around me—with the policeman, the wreck, the workers with crowbars trying to liberate me, the ambulance, the flowers on a nearby hedge, and the television cameraman. Somewhere I could see and feel my injuries, but they did not seem to have anything to do with me; they were merely a part of a rapidly expanding network that included much more than my body. The sunlight was unusually bright and golden and the entire world seemed to shimmer with a beautiful radiance. I felt blissful and exuberant, even in the middle of the drama around me, and I remained in that state for several days in the hospital.

The accident and the experience that accompanied it totally transformed my worldview and my way of understanding existence. Previously, I had not had much interest in spiritual areas and my concept of life was that it was contained between birth and death. The thought of death always frightened me. I had believed that "We walk across life's stage but once," and then—nothing. Consequently I had been driven by the fear that I would not have a chance to do all that I wanted to accomplish during my life. Now, the world and my place in it feel completely different. I feel that my self-definition transcends the notion of a limited physical body existing in a limited time frame. I know myself to be part of a larger, unrestricted, creative network that could be described as divine.[1]

Despite the many books and articles published on pre-death and near-death experiences from the turn of the century onward, it was the 1975 publication of Dr. Raymond Moody's *Life After Life* that began a new phase of research into the visions of the dying. Moody first learned about NDEs from Dr. George Ritchie, whom he met in 1965 while studying philosophy as an undergraduate at the University of Virginia. Ritchie, a former army doctor and resident psychiatrist in the School of Medicine at Virginia, spoke openly about an NDE he underwent in 1943 while serving as a private in the army. As he tells it in his book about the experience, *Return from Tomorrow*, he contracted double lobar pneumonia, went into cardiac arrest, and apparently died. However, nine minutes after being pronounced dead, someone decided to inject him with Adrenalin and he came back to life. What occurred in those nine minutes would change Dr. Ritchie's life, because during this time he said that he left his body, underwent a dramatic life-review process, experienced the light of heaven, and reluctantly made the decision to return to his body in order to "become a physician so that I could learn about man and then serve God." After hearing Dr. Ritchie recount this story, Moody came away impressed. The seed of interest had been planted.

By 1972, Dr. Moody had taken a Ph.D. in philosophy and had entered medical school with the aim of teaching the philosophy of medicine. At the same time he also began collecting stories from men and women who had undergone experiences similar to Dr. Ritchie's. Within two years he had collected 150 accounts of NDEs. Although many of the cases he studied involved revival from apparent, or "clinical," death, Dr. Moody meant the term "near-death experience" to include the variety of unusual episodes reported by individuals who had survived life-threatening dangers without being physically harmed. NDEs, in other words, need not be restricted to experiences on operating tables but to anyone who has been faced with grave physical danger. From the mass of anecdotal material he collected, Moody isolated the most common elements of the NDE, principal among them: the sensations of floating out of one's body; passing through a dark tunnel; ascending toward a bright light; meetings with friends and relatives; a panoramic life review; a reluctance to return to the body; an unusual perception of time and space; and a sense of disappointment at being revived.

During the course of his research, Moody also noted that the common elements he identified tended to occur in a somewhat predictable pattern, confirming the researches of Heim, Osis, Noyes, and Kletti. On the basis of these points of likeness, and consistent with the pattern of progression he typically saw, Moody created a composite NDE, or what he termed a "theoretically ideal or complete experience." Because this composite portrait has played such a significant role in shaping contemporary NDE research, I quote it here in its entirety:

A man is dying, and as he reaches the point of greatest physical distress, he hears himself pronounced dead by his doctor. He begins to hear an uncomfortable noise, a loud ringing or buzzing, and at the same time feels himself moving very rapidly through a long dark tunnel. After this, he suddenly feels himself outside of his own physical body, but still in the immediate physical environment, and he sees his own body from a distance, as though he is a spectator. He watches the resuscitation attempt from this unusual vantage point and is in a state of emotional upheaval.

After a while, he collects himself and becomes more

accustomed to his odd condition. He notices that he still has a "body," but one of a very different nature and with very different powers from the physical body he has left behind. Soon other things begin to happen. Others come to meet and to help him. He glimpses the spirits of relatives and friends who have already died, and a loving, warm spirit of a kind he has never encountered before— a being of light—appears before him. This being asks him a question, nonverbally, to make him evaluate his life and helps him along by showing him a panoramic, instantaneous playback of the major events of his life. At some point he finds himself approaching some sort of barrier or border, apparently representing the limit between earthly life and the next life. Yet, he finds that he must go back to earth, that the time for his death has not yet come. At this point he resists, for by now he is taken up with his experiences in the afterlife and does not want to return. He is overwhelmed by intense feelings of joy, love, and peace. Despite his attitude, though, he somehow reunites with his physical body and lives.

Later he tries to tell others, but he has trouble doing so. In the first place, he can find no human words adequate to describe these unearthly episodes. He also finds that others scoff, so he stops telling other people. Still, the experience affects his life profoundly, especially his views about death and its relationship to life.[2]

Dr. Moody was careful to stress that not a single person he interviewed reported experiencing each and every one of these elements, or that every NDE progresses in exactly this manner. But he was impressed with, as he put it, "the striking similarities among the accounts of the experiences themselves." So too were a great many others, because Moody's research inspired an entire new generation of NDE researchers, the most prominent among them Dr. Kenneth Ring (a psychologist who produced a large, systematic study of NDEs that confirmed the bulk of Moody's findings), Dr. Michael B. Sabom (a cardiologist who sought to verify Moody's findings scientifically), and Dr. Melvin Moorse (who conducted a large-scale study of the NDEs of children). Along with a host of others, these researchers arrived at the following conclusions regarding NDEs.

1. While it is nearly impossible to verify whether or not people who have had NDEs actually return from death, it is undeniable that NDEs occur regularly worldwide. As I noted earlier, George Gallup estimates that some eight million Americans have had NDEs. In the same poll, Gallup also analyzed the elements people most commonly experienced in NDEs. Here is what he found:

Element	Percent of those who have had NDEs who experience it
Out-of-body experience	26
Accurate visual perception	23
Audible sounds or voices	17
Feelings of peace, painlessness	32
Light phenomena	14
Life review	32
Being in another world	32
Encountering other beings	23
Tunnel experience	9
Precognition	6

2. The vast majority of those who have had near-death experiences do not as a rule fear death, and this loss of fear is nearly permanent. However, near-death experiencers seldom say they have lost all fear of the process of dying—it is only death they no longer fear.

3. A very small number of NDEs are negative, in which people say they experience torment rather than peace and joy. (I will explore this subject in detail in Chapter 5.)

4. As Dr. Melvin Moorse has shown in *Closer to the Light*, NDEs are not limited to adults; they also occur for children, many of whom are quite young.

5. Approximately 35 percent of those who come close to death will have an NDE.

6. NDEs appear to be a natural psychological process associated with dying. However, opinions vary widely as to what exactly triggers them.

Many psychologists, among them Dr. Russell Noyes, Jr., and Dr. Roy Kletti, have adopted what has come to be called the "depersonalization theory," which hypothesizes that the prospect of death sets in motion a defensive psychological reaction that enables people to cope with the stress of life-threatening situations. A handful of research physicians have been drawn to pharmacological explanations, the most popular of which simply holds that NDEs are triggered by the anesthetics given to patients in hospitals. Another popular theory is neurologically based, holding that NDEs are caused by the seizure-like neural firing patterns created in the temporal lobe of the brain.

Several other possible explanations have been put forward to explain the cause of NDEs, but to date not a single theory has been able to stand up to serious scrutiny. All that can be said with certainty at the present time is that we just don't know what causes NDEs. (For additional information on this subject, please refer to the bibliography at the end of this book.)

7. NDEs appear to be culturally conditioned. Hindus, for example, are likely to encounter the gods Vishnu or Shiva

in their near-death visions, while Christians will encounter Christ. Agnostics tend most often to describe a light or a presence that is lovely and wondrous.

8. NDEs are transformative events insofar as the majority of people who return from one are never the same again. In the main, these transformations are positive, powerful, and spiritually enriching.

9. While there are several common elements to NDEs, no two experiences are identical.

These facts and statistics about NDEs do not prove the existence of life after death. As I said before, this is a debate that the living will probably never reach a consensus about. Once again, as is so often the case with the things that matter most, faith remains crucial.

For the seeker of truth, the courage to believe will always remain equally as important as the courage to doubt. This is why I believe that the stories of those who have had near-death experiences are so important, as they provide us with tantalizing hints of what may lie in store for us on the other side of life. They are, if nothing else, powerful seeds of hope for those who find it easier to doubt than to believe. Near-death experiences are also gifts, or clues from God, that there may be "something afoot in the universe," as Pierre Teilhard de Chardin put it, "something that looks like gestation and birth." Something, in other words, that looks like purpose, hope, and love.

Even for those who are inclined to relish their doubts, it is still a mistake to write off the extraordinary claims of near-death experiencers too quickly. For much of what they have told us about life after death, time and eternity, is rooted not only in religious philosophy but in contemporary physics. After all, was it not Einstein who proved to us that time does not begin or end, but constitutes a continuum in infinite space? If we can believe that much, then the stories of those who have had near-death experiences should sound a great deal less far-fetched to us, for what they describe is a journey so long and so magnificent that we can't begin to visualize it, let alone explain it.

Dylan Thomas may have found it necessary to implore his dying father to "rage against the dying of the light," but I see no reason why any of us should feel compelled to adopt his advice. For now we know that the light may be turned up again in another room, and by all accounts the scenery and the company that await us will be nothing short of glorious. This was certainly so for the many near-death experiencers I have met, and as I plan to show in the following chapters, it was also the case for many of our ancestors.

PART TWO
JOURNEYS OF THE SOUL—PAST AND PRESENT

4

THE FLIGHT OF THE SOUL

∞

As the moon dieth and cometh to life again, so we also, having to die, will rise again.
—San Juan Capistrano Indians of California

Then with no fiery, throbbing pain,
No cold gradation of decay,
Death broke at once the vital chain,
And freed his soul the nearest way.
—Samuel Johnson

I have lost many loved ones in my life, yet I often feel they've never really left me. My father, for example, died some twenty years ago yet I think of him quite often, most recently while I was reading one of his favorite books, Daniel J. Boorstin's 1948 classic, *The Lost World of Thomas Jefferson.*

One thing that intrigued me about Jefferson was that he refused to say much about the subject of death, even though he was a deeply reflective man. He managed to hold his tongue on the subject all the way up until his eighty-third birthday, when at last he declared himself ready for the final adventure, "untried by the living and unreported by the dead." When I first encountered this line my immediate reaction was one of amused delight, for it appears that Jefferson (as, no doubt, my father) was unaware of the fact that men and women had actually been reporting experiences of returning from death long before he penned his famous signature on the Constitution. A great many scholars even believe that the great Saint Paul hinted in Jefferson's copy of the Bible that he was once privileged with a flight to heaven:

> I know a man in Christ who fourteen years ago was caught up to the third heaven—whether in the body or out of the body I do not know, God knows. And I know that this man was caught up into Paradise—whether in the body or out of the body I do not know, God knows— and he heard things that cannot be told, which man may not utter. (2 Corinthians 12:2–4)

Saint Paul's oblique reference to himself and his journey to heaven is just one of many historical parallels to contemporary NDEs left to us from history. Yet I'm pretty certain Jefferson would have questioned the validity of Paul's near-death story, or any near-death account for that matter. In keeping with the intellectual spirit of his time, he was a deist; a man of reason who believed in God yet placed little credence in spiritual revelations. In this sense, Jefferson was not unlike my father, and millions of people today, for in an age dominated by science, agnosticism comes easier than faith.

However, just a few hundred years before Jefferson's time, few people on earth shared his perspective, for nearly every ancient culture promoted the belief that death is not the absolute and irrevocable end of human existence; that consciousness, or life, in some form or another continues on after the demise of our physical bodies. This view was passionately presented in the idealistic writings of Plato, who said that death is nothing more than a change, "a migration of the soul from this place to another." This same belief was also promoted in the Judaic, Christian, Moslem, and Egyptian traditions, as well as in the Eastern traditions of Buddhism and Hinduism.

These ancient religious and mythological traditions differed widely in the details of the nature of the soul's flight after death. Yet they all agreed that death was nothing more than a transition, a progression, and not the final annihilation of the individual. Ralph Waldo Emerson and Henry David Thoreau knew this. Within five years of Jefferson's death in 1826, they had already begun to immerse themselves in the literature of many ancient cultures, seeking to confirm their intuition that we are not here alone, nor for ourselves alone, but are actually an integral part of something much larger, much nobler, and far more mysterious and lovely than we can comprehend or possibly describe in words. Eventually, through a combination of meditation, reflection, and study, each came to believe in the light of eternal life. As Thoreau would write, "Let nothing stand between you and the light. . . . When you travel to the celestial city, carry no letter of introduction. When you knock, ask to see God. . . ."

Fortunately, access to these ancient traditions has not been lost to us. In fact, due to a wealth of high-quality translations and recent archeological finds, we are even freer to explore these traditions today than were Emerson and Thoreau. And when we do, we find a surprising number of accounts of NDEs, the most detailed of which were preserved for us by the many ambitious monks of medieval Europe. Here and in the following four chapters I will explore some of these intriguing historical parallels as I break down the various elements of the NDE. While my primary focus will remain with the insights of the near-death experiencers I interviewed firsthand, I will occasionally compare their testimonies to a few of the many near-death stories preserved for us from our distant past. At the same time, I will also briefly survey the mythology of death as it has been understood by many ancient civilizations since the dawn of human history. We begin with the flight of the soul itself.

EXIT FROM THE BODY

In a culture such as ours, which prizes youth and beauty over age and wisdom, it isn't surprising that the majority of us tend to identify ourselves with our physical bodies. But this is not the case with those who have had near-death experiences. As a result of their out-of-body experiences, most of them become convinced that at the moment of death, a spirit, or soul, departs our bodies. The actual process of this flight of the soul has varied somewhat over the course of history, but there is little question among those who have undergone NDEs that a nearly indescribable *something* floats up and away from our bodies at the moment of death.

For most of the experiencers I interviewed, this unexpected departure of the soul was quite shocking, and this is easily understandable. Many, like Dr. George Rodonaia, were taken by complete surprise: "I wasn't prepared for this at all. I was shocked to find that I still existed, but I didn't know who or what I was. The one thought that kept rolling through my mind was, How can I be when I'm not?"

Although I met one near-death experiencer who told me that her soul slowly slipped away in a long and somewhat agonizing process, the majority of those I spoke with said they left their bodies almost effortlessly; the process was swift, peaceful, and painless. At one point they were filled with pain and fear and fully conscious of residing in their body, the next they were free from pain, full of peace, and looking down at "themselves." John Wintek, a retired army sergeant from Kentucky who was pronounced clinically dead after his aorta ruptured in 1981, described his out-of-body experience to me this way:

I was lying in bed in an army hospital at Fort Knox when my main aorta blew out. The first thing I remember was seeing this amazing array of concise, unbelievable colors, which filled me with a tremendous sense of serenity. I also remember that I had the sensation of just floating around in the middle of it all. Then, as I was drinking in all this beauty, I looked down and saw six people in white robes working over this outstretched figure who was just flapping and jerking around on a bed, as though he had lost all control over himself. The people were moving about very frantically too, as though they were in a panic. I had no sense at the time that they were working on me, so I just redirected my attention back to all this beauty, and to this great warm light that was radiating in the distance—this light, this light, oh my goodness, did I want to go to this light! I wanted to be with it.

But then I looked down again, and I can't say when or how long this all took to occur, because I had no sense of time at all. But I could see that the white-robed figures were moving more slowly, and that the body on the bed had grown still and quiet. That's when it hit me that I was the body on the bed. Or maybe I should say that the body on the bed is what my "I" had just departed from. They were bringing out these paddles to restart my heart, and I remember that I was trying somehow to communicate to them that they shouldn't bother with that, that I was okay, and that I much preferred to stay where I was. My whole focus at the time was on God. I just wanted to stay with God.

My surgeon and anesthesiologist confirmed to me after my NDE that this is exactly what occurred. There were six of them in the room, they were initially in a state of panic, and they brought me back to my body with heart paddles.

Another near-death experiencer I spoke with, Dorothy Bernstein, told me she felt herself pulled from her body by the hand of God:

I was at St. John's Hospital in Cleveland. I originally went in for a hysterectomy in February of 1972. Then I had to go back three weeks later because I contracted pneumonia and pleurisy. They didn't know if it was viral pneumonia or bacterial pneumonia, so they isolated me in the bishop's special room; very austere, you know, no TV, just a small bed and two chests. And of course there was a cross over the bed, facing north, toward Lake Erie.

I remember that a nurse gave me medication at six o'clock. I told her that it wasn't working, that I didn't want to take it, but I went ahead and swallowed it anyway just to make her happy. No sooner had I done so than I found it difficult to breathe. It seemed as though my lungs were coated with thick fluid and clogged up, because I couldn't get any air. I tried pounding my ribs, trying to open them, but no luck. I asked the nurse to call the doctors, but they were having supper and were not to be disturbed except in emergencies. I said, "This is an emergency!" but the nurse didn't think so. Then I remember saying to the nurse, "My God, I can't believe it. I'm in a Catholic hospital and I'm dying."

"In that case," the nurse said, "I can give you another medication." I told her it was too late, but I took it anyway.

At this point, I knew I was going to die. I couldn't breathe. Then I just leaned back on the pillow, closed my eyes, and said, "Oh God, is this to be my punishment? Must I die alone, without my God?" Then I felt my left

70

wrist grabbed, just like a human hand, and I was jerked right out through my head and out of the bed. At the same time I heard a popping noise, like a champagne cork popping out of a bottle. Then I heard a voice say, "When did I ever punish you?" I knew instantly it was the voice of God.

Then I began reviewing my life as God carried me up and away from the earth, traveling on a beam of light to the total brightness ahead. Before we hit the light, I heard the nurse say, "Open your eyes." I said, "No, I want to see what is in the light." Then I looked down and saw that my mouth was moving, so I said to my body, "Why are you talking? You are dead." It wasn't until this time that I came to realize that my whole body didn't come along with me, only my soul. And I must tell you, I never felt so young and so healthy and so happy in my life. That God actually came to get me and lift me to his light was just unbelievable. I was ecstatic.

Dorothy Bernstein's description of having her soul "jerked" from her body by the hand of God is enormously similar to many near-death accounts left to us from history. For, like Dorothy, several near-death experiencers from the distant past said that angels, relatives, or animal spirits came to aid them in their transition at death.

In the history of Christian near-death testimony, angelic assistance at the moment of death is commonly described. An excellent example appears in the near-death story of Salvius, a sixth-century Christian priest who reported that he returned from an NDE after spending an entire evening lifeless on a funeral bier:

Four days ago, I died and was taken by two angels to the height of heaven ... Then I went through a gate that was brighter than normal daylight, into a place where the en-

tire floor shone like gold and silver. The light was indescribable, and I can't tell you how vast it was.

Similar encounters with angels were reported by numerous medieval Christian near-death experiencers. For example, a seventh-century monk named Barontus reported that
"[the archangel] Raphael touched my throat and I . . . suddenly sensed my soul torn out of my body." In Egypt, a
desert monk, whose NDE story was recorded in the third
or fourth century, noted that at the time of his death he was
met by the angels Gabriel and Michael, whom the Lord had
sent together with a chorus singing songs of praise for God.
While he was initially reluctant to leave his body, when he
heard their voices he no longer felt any need to hang on. It
was then, he said, that "my soul came forth into the hands
of Michael and was carried up with joy."

In one of the most dramatic near-death stories ever recorded, Black Elk, a Lakota Sioux holy man, reported that
he was similarly assisted in the process of departing his
ailing body. His angels, however, came in the form of "thunder beings," who descended like lightning from the clouds.
The details of his powerful NDE were painstakingly recorded by John G. Neihardt and published in 1931 in his
spiritual classic, *Black Elk Speaks*. As we learn in this book,
Black Elk's NDE occurred at the age of nine, while he was
journeying up the Platte River with his family, en route to
the Colorado Rockies. One morning, after jumping off his
horse to get a drink of water from a creek, he was suddenly
seized by a severe paralysis in his legs. Two days later, after
being pulled by his horse for many hours in a pony drag,
he became terribly ill. His arms, legs, and face had swollen
so badly that he found it difficult to move. As he lay dying
in his tepee with his mother and father beside him, he suddenly left his body:

I could see out through the opening [of the tepee], and there two men were coming from the clouds, heading first like arrows slanting down. . . . Each carried a long spear, and from the points of these a jagged lightning flashed. They came clear down to the ground . . . and stood a little way off and looked at me and said: "Hurry! Come! Your Grandfathers are calling you!"

Then they turned and left the ground like arrows slanting upward from the bow. When I got up to follow, my legs did not hurt anymore and I was very light. I went outside the tepee, and yonder where the men with flaming spears were going, a little cloud was coming very fast. It came and stooped and took me and turned back to where it came from, flying fast. And when I looked down I could see my mother and father yonder, and I felt sorry to be leaving them.

Then there was nothing but the air and the swiftness of the little cloud that bore me and those two men still leading up to where white clouds were piled like mountains on a wide blue plain, and in them thunder beings lived and leaped and flashed.

Black Elk's encounter with thunder beings is unusual, because in early non-Christian mythological traditions, it is more often the "soulbird" who appears to aid the deceased at the moment of departure. Birds have long been a universal symbol of the soul. In the mythologies of Egyptians, Parsees, Scythians, and North American Indians, eagles, hawks, and thunderbirds were said to appear at the moment of death to serve as spirit guides—messengers who were able to fly between the worlds of the living and the dead. In Greek, Roman, and Nordic mythologies, the swan or gander was said to appear to aid the departed in their transition at death.

NATURE OF THE SOUL

When Raymond Moody first began studying NDEs in the 1970s, he coined the term "spiritual body" to describe the nature of the disembodied soul. He chose this term because the many near-death experiencers he interviewed told him that when their souls departed their bodies they felt as though they were no longer fully physical beings, yet neither were they totally ethereal. They lived in a third state, which many of them could describe only as "pure consciousness."

Of the many near-death experiencers I have met, most felt they took on a new body of some sort, tending to describe that body as a cloud, a sphere, or some form of light. Moody's use of the term "spiritual body" therefore seems as good a name for the out-of-body soul as any. It is a sufficiently broad term to do justice to the many attempts those who have had near-death experiences have made to describe what it feels to be out-of-body. Here is what near-death experiencer John Wintek told me:

When I left my body I had no sense of feeling the same sensations that we normally feel here on earth, and that is why it is so hard for me to describe the nature of soul. Everything I felt or came to know was communicated to me spiritually, so it was not as though I saw things like I did on earth, or heard things as I did on earth, or felt things as I did on earth. I gained a new kind of knowledge unlike any I had ever experienced. I had no sense of motion, either; there was no up and down, or moving my body parts to see or look. For example, when I looked down to see my body in the hospital bed, I did not physically have to look down. I just saw all this. I had no sense that I moved my body or head. And as I told you before, I felt like I was floating. It was a feeling of complete freedom, complete joy—unboundedness, I guess, is a good way to put it. That is the best way to describe the soul, unbounded and free. The only thing that troubled me at all about this experience was that I had to come back down and reenter my body, because I don't know what more I could have experienced in terms of feeling, in terms of joy. It was a feeling of utter and complete belonging, a feeling of being loved by all, connected to all, as though I had finally arrived home after a long and difficult journey.

I asked Dr. George Rodonaia, whose story appears in Chapter Two, to elaborate for me what it felt like for him to be out-of-body:

When you leave your body you are not in time, and you feel a sense of lightness. *Lightness* is the word that comes to my mind. As the ego slips away, as the awareness of gross matter slips away, gravity disappears entirely and you feel light like a feather. You enter into another dimension. Being without a body is about lightness, freedom, comfort, relaxation. At first, of course, you are afraid, because you lose some of your normal senses. But you gain an entire fresh set of senses, and they open a whole new world of beauty and experience such as you never thought possible.

Our ancestors encountered much the same difficulty when trying to describe the nature of their out-of-body souls. In the third century, for example, an Egyptian who had had a near-death experience named Zosimus arrived at the conclusion that those who depart their bodies at death "see the shape of the soul as a shape of light, perfect in all the body apart from the distinction of male and female." The seventh-century monk Barontus, who was struck down by a nearly fatal fever in the monastery where he lived, said that "my little soul . . . could not speak until, when it came time for discussion, it received a body of air similar to the one I had left behind." He went on to say that his soul "seemed so small that it was like a tiny bird just hatched from the egg." In *The Dialogue of Miracles*, the medieval abbot Caesarius of Heisterbach writes that he discovered, in the course of his NDE, that the soul is molded like "a glassy spherical vessel, with eyes before and behind, all-knowing and seeing everything at once." Another unknown near-death experiencer, whose story was recorded by Caesarius, said that his soul was "a spiritual substance, spherical in nature, like the globe of the moon."

WHAT SURVIVES?

Since there is broad agreement among those who have had near-death experiences that a soul departs our bodies at death, an intriguing question arises: What will consciousness, or soulfulness, be like on the other side of life? For the strictly materialistically minded person, this is an easy question to answer. After the physical brain shuts down, there is nothing to look forward to but silence. But for those who operate with a bit more faith, this is a vital, living question. As an elderly man once explained to me, "I am pretty sure I possess an eternal soul. What I'm not at all sure about is what life will be like when I leave my body. As I get older, I wonder about this more and more."

Dr. Charles Tart, professor emeritus of psychology at the University of California at Davis, has wondered about this a great deal himself. After three decades of research in the field of parapsychology, and the analysis of thousands of experiments, he is now firmly convinced that "there are aspects of the human mind that simply cannot be reduced to materialistic explanations." Therefore, he says, "consciousness can exist independently of the body."

What especially intrigues Dr. Tart is the form this consciousness will take when we die. In his view, it will in all likelihood be quite different from the consciousness we experience while we are attached to our bodies, for the simple reason that we gain a sense of who we are through the input of our many senses. In other words, once those senses are shed, our perception of who we are, and how we experience our relationship with the wider universe, is surely going to change. "Thus," he writes, "although we should not be too surprised if we regain some sort of consciousness after death, by the same token we should not be too surprised if that consciousness is considerably—perhaps profoundly—different from the ordinary state of waking consciousness to which we were accustomed during life." Fortunately, by all accounts this new form of consciousness has many surprising features, not the least of which is the ability to travel almost effortlessly toward an enchanting white light.

THE TUNNNEL

In the popular imagination, NDEs are generally associated with a journey down a long, dark tunnel toward a brilliant, white light. Yet in my own studies of modern and ancient near-death stories, I have encountered very few accounts of "tunnel travel." It appears the experience of traveling in a tunnel is actually quite rare. Gallup reports that of those who have had an NDE, only 10 percent actually describe such a journey.

For those who actually do enter the tunnel, however, the experience is quite affecting. Typically, the tunnel is entered

shortly after the out-of-body experience. But one man I interviewed, Andy Petro, entered the tunnel instantly. His NDE
occurred in the summer of 1956, when he was seventeen.
He had gone with some high school friends to the shores
of Lake Michigan, and as he was swimming out to a floating
dock, his legs began to cramp. When he cried out for help,
his friends didn't respond because (as he later learned) they
thought he was playing a prank on them. After struggling
to keep himself afloat with his hands, Andy eventually descended to the bottom of the lake. As he told me:

> After I landed on the bottom, the first thing I felt was all
> this muck—the mud and the muck and the reeds at the
> bottom of the lake. I was down probably fifteen to twenty
> feet, because I was not all that far from shore. Maybe one
> hundred, two hundred yards. I was in a state of complete
> terror, and was very cold, because [as you go deeper] in
> the lake, the temperature really drops off fast. My legs
> were so paralyzed that there was just no way I was going
> to be able to swim to the surface. I was gonna die. And I
> was full of pain. I was frozen and terrified. Every muscle
> in my body was screaming out with pain. And I'm done,
> you know.
>
>   Then all of a sudden in my head I heard myself say, "I
> need to rest. There is no way I can go on. I'm in so much
> pain, I need to rest." So somehow, on the bottom of that
> lake, I talked myself into letting go, and as soon as I let
> go, the next instant, I was in the tunnel. The letting-go
> process sent me shooting down this tunnel. It was dark
> and spherical, and as I entered it, I could see myself at
> the bottom of the lake. So I knew that the Andy now
> entering the tunnel was the same Andy that was stuck on
> the bottom of the lake. That connection was there. Initially
> it was a bit frightening, but my first thought was, Boy, it
> sure is great to be warm. I was no longer cold and I no

longer felt any pain. So my fear just lifted. I could see this light at the far end of the tunnel feeding warmth to me. It was the beginning of a euphoric feeling. And the closer I got to the light, as I shot down this tunnel, the warmer I got.

Andy was eventually rescued by his friends and resuscitated on a nearby shore.

Despite a tremendous amount of digging, I have found very few premodern near-death accounts that actually describe a tunnel experience similar to Andy's. Sir Owen, a tenth-century English knight whose near-death account is recorded in the *Treatise on the Purgatory of St. Patrick* (composed by the twelfth-century English Cistercian monk, H. of San Ivy), said that he traveled down a tunnel in his NDE, but the tunnel he described was actually a long, dark passageway, something more akin to a cave or an underground canal than the spherical tube described by contemporaries. The only significant hint that tunnel experiences may have occurred in earlier times is found in the work of the fifteenth-century artist Hieronymus Bosch. His famous painting *Ascent into the Empyrean* is a nearly perfect illustration of the long spherical tunnel described by modern-day near-death experiencers. Another strikingly similar rendition of a tunnel was composed in the nineteenth century by Gustave Doré to serve as an illustration to Dante's *Paradiso*.

GUIDES

According to pollster George Gallup, 23 percent of those who undergo NDEs today encounter other people after they leave their bodies, although seldom at the instant of departure as so often happened for premodern people who had

near-death experiences. Most often, these people arrive after
the soul has left the body, generally appearing in the form
of deceased relatives or "spiritual beings." Whether these
relatives or spiritual beings actually speak to near-death experiencers verbally or communicate with them telepathi-
cally, they nearly always appear as reassuring presences.
They also help guide experiencers through the afterlife,
pointing out the meaning of the many signs and symbols
along the way.

Carol Larson, a woman from California who underwent
a near-death experience, described for me how she was
guided toward the light by her deceased mother:

> I was a bit scared at first, as I guess we all must be when
> we die. But when I saw the light my fear went away pretty
> fast. And I remember that as I was approaching the light
> I saw my mother, Heidi, who died about ten years ago
> from lung cancer. She wasn't smiling or anything like
> that—you know, like she was greeting me at the airport
> or something. But she had this look of quiet calm, of peace,
> and she was radiating all this love to me. She took my
> hand and somehow made it clear to me that I had nothing
> to fear. She told me that I could approach the light and it
> wouldn't hurt me. But she also said that I would have to
> go back. All I felt from her was love and understanding.
> It felt wonderful.

Carol's experience of encountering a relative who would
befriend and guide her through the process of death is commonly reported in contemporary NDEs. Less common are
those who report the aid of angels, saints, or other powerful
spiritual figures. In the course of my research, I encountered
only a few such experiences. Elaine Durham, whose NDE
was precipitated by a heart seizure she suffered shortly after

receiving the last sacrament rites from a priest at a Chicago hospital in 1976, shared with me the following story:

> I felt this tremendous brightness emerge next to my side, and I instantly knew that Christ was walking beside me. I can't consciously tell you that I saw his face, and yet I know that I did. For me to sit here and say he had this kind of hair, or these color of eyes, well, I can't tell you this, because that part of it has been taken from my memory. But the whiteness from what he wore was more radiant than anything I can possibly describe—a spun white glow that just radiated off of him. And there was a warmth of love that just permeated everything. He then let me know that he was taking me to a point where everything would be explained to me. Eventually, we arrived at a mountain, and he turned me over to an angel, who began to explain to me the meaning of life and death.

The majority of medieval people who had NDEs also felt they were guided after death. Very seldom, however, were those guides deceased relatives. Their guides nearly always came as spiritual beings such as those described by Elaine Durham, most commonly their favorite saints or angels. Often they said that the same angel who came to help them in the process of departing from their body accompanied them for the remainder of their journey through the afterlife. In nearly every instance, these guides are portrayed as luminous figures of beauty and wisdom—shining, kindly personages dressed in brilliant white robes. As Drythelm, an eighth-century Northumbrian man who died one evening from a severe illness but sat up abruptly before his mourners on the following day at dawn, reported: "I was guided by someone of shining countenance and bright apparel."

Interestingly, angelic guides appear far more frequently in the near-death stories of children than they do in the accounts of contemporary adults. In his engaging study of the NDEs of children, *Closer to the Light,* Dr. Melvin Moorse relates the near-death story of a boy named Kurt, a seven-year-old patient who suffered from a severe case of muscular dystrophy. Kurt's condition deteriorated to the point that he went into a seizure in the intensive-care unit. Dr. Moorse reports that Kurt's heart stopped and he was without a heartbeat for three minutes. Kurt later told Dr. Moorse that during this time he found himself outside his body watching the doctors and nurses who were working to revive him. He also said that he was greeted by angels when his soul left his body and that he met many people. And, like Elaine Durham, he also reported encountering Jesus:

> I saw Bonnie [one of the nurses present], and I said hi to her. Then everything became dark, until I saw angels. I was in a beautiful place with flowers and rainbows, where everything was white, like it had its own light. I talked to several people while I was there, including Jesus, who wanted me to stay with him. I wanted to stay there, but we decided I had to come back and see my parents again. I'm not afraid to go back to that place.[1]

For contemporary experiencers like Kurt, friends, relatives, and spiritual guides appear primarily in order to provide them with comfort, to ease them into the process of death, and, as we shall later see, to help them through the life-review process. For those who have had near-death experiences in the past, guides served a similar function; but they also often served an important additional function: they occasionally took them on a guided tour of hell.

5

TO HELL AND BACK

∞

Even though I walk through the valley of the shadow of death,
I fear no evil; for you are with me.

—Psalms (23:4)

Be not fond of the dull, smoke-colored light from hell.

—Tibetan Book of the Dead

When, as a young boy, I was first introduced to the concept of hell by a TV cartoon, I remember it troubled me so deeply I couldn't sleep in the dark for months afterward. I had to keep a night-light on, and the door to my bedroom had to be open so I could look out into the hall. Somehow, I came to associate darkness with hell, and hell to me meant pesky little men in red tights who were always out to stab you with their pitchforks. They threw fireballs at you, screamed at you, and just generally went out of their way to make your life miserable.

I was hardly alone in my fears, because I eventually learned that the concept of hell has long been a universal theme in the world's religious and mythological traditions. While traveling the United States in the 1980s, I also came to see that hell continues to exert a powerful influence on the thinking of millions of people today. A recent poll conducted by *USA Today*, CNN, and the Gallup organization found that 90 percent of Americans believe in hell, and that 65 percent believe in the devil. I must say that these statistics are the highest I have ever seen reported, and certainly prove that the idea of hell is alive and thriving in America.

Given that most Americans believe in hell, it is difficult to understand why just one of the near-death experiencers I spoke with reported having a negative, or "hellish," experience. More often, the people I met told me that their experiences were warm, joyous, and overwhelmingly affirmative. Nevertheless, nothing precludes the possibility of a negative NDE, and I have heard of a few such experiences in recent years.

The first contemporary writer to argue that hellish NDEs exist—and that they are actually quite common—is Dr. Maurice Rawlings, a practicing cardiologist. In his 1978 book on the subject, *Beyond Death's Door*, he claims to have resuscitated several men and women who had hellish NDEs. Although Dr. Rawlings' book has been heavily criticized by scholars for its questionable research methodology and because he used negative near-death accounts as a tool for Christian evangelism, few researchers today doubt that negative experiences occasionally occur. The question is, why do they occur? And why are they so very rare in our time?

The most dramatic hellish NDE I have encountered is that of former art professor Howard Storm. I first learned about Storm as he retold his story at a near-death support group in Cincinnati. Storm's NDE occurred on June 1, 1985, while he was in Paris on the last day of a European summer tour he had been conducting for art students. I quote his experience at length here not only because his story is unusually compelling, but because it sheds tremendous light on the nature of hellish NDEs.

What I am about to describe to you is the person that I was prior to my NDE. It is not pleasant for me to talk about myself this way, because, looking back, I see that it is a very unflattering picture.

By society's standards, I was doing very well prior to my NDE. I was a professor of art at North Kentucky University, chairperson of the art department, and I had a lovely wife and a family and two cars. I had it all. Inwardly, though, I used to think about killing myself a lot because I didn't really find joy in anything. Everything to me was an extension of my ego, and I basically liked what I could control and despised what I couldn't. I was really a very lonely and selfish man.

I had no faith in anything that couldn't be seen, touched, or felt. I believed only in the material world, and I knew with certainty it was the full extent of everything there was. I considered all religions, and all belief systems, fantasies for people to deceive themselves with. But I felt that if people needed those fantasies, why, that was okay. But *I* didn't. *I* believed in what science said, that everything was measurable and that we were in the process of finishing up our discovery of all known reality. Through our ability to control nature, science was going to create a wonderful world of abundance for everyone.

All of these views were severely challenged on June 1, 1985, when I had my NDE. This was to be the second to the last day of our summer trip to Europe, and we had a few students along, whom we were taking to museums, theaters, castles, etcetera. Anyway, it was Saturday morning and I was talking to a student, and all of a sudden I felt an intense stabbing pain in the center of my abdominal area. It hit with such severity that I crumpled up and fell to the floor screaming. I was full of fear and anxiety. I yelled at my wife to get a doctor. The doctor immediately gave me morphine to relieve the pain and I was soon racing through Paris in an ambulance at fifty to sixty miles per hour.

When we got to the hospital, they said I had a perforation in my small intestine. I asked if I could fly to the U.S. to have the operation done there, but they said it was impossible. I needed to be operated on soon because I was in a grave situation. They then put me in a room where I spent the next several hours waiting to be operated on. And as I was waiting, the morphine slowly wore off and I felt this excruciating pain, ten times worse than when it first hit me. The pain was just so incredible I couldn't understand why I was still conscious. Nobody can endure such pain and remain conscious, that is the thought that kept running through my head. Why am I conscious? I wanted to black out, but I couldn't. So I told the guy in the bed next to me—a man named Michel Fleurian, who spoke English—to tell the nurse that I'm gonna die real soon if something doesn't happen. Tell them I need morphine. And he did that, but nothing happened.

My wife was frantically trying to get the hospital to do something, but was totally ineffectual. The nurse came in around eight P.M. to tell me that the doctor had gone home but would operate on me the next day, Sunday, in the morning. I didn't say anything, because I knew that was my death sentence. I was shot. I knew I wouldn't survive, because the pain I was in was beyond description. I told my wife I loved her very much, because I sensed this was the end. Then I tried to relax and closed my eyes, waiting for the big nothing of death. I mean, I was waiting for the big zero, the big blackout, the one we never wake up from, the end of existence, which I knew and felt with absolute certainty was the way it was. It never occurred to me to pray; never once during that entire afternoon. I was a grown-up, and grown-ups don't need to pray. I never mentioned God's name, except, perhaps, in a moment of profanity. I'd never had a problem taking the Lord's name in vain, you know.

I slipped off into a state of unconsciousness, and I don't know how long it lasted. I felt real strange, so I opened my eyes, and to my surprise I was standing up next to the bed looking down at my body in the bed. My first reaction was, This is crazy! You can't be standing here looking down at yourself. This is not possible. I was angry and upset, so I started yelling and screaming at my wife, even swearing obscenities at her, but she just sat there like a stone. She wouldn't move. I'm yelling and screaming at her, but nothing. And I can't tell you, because it was just all profanities that I was saying, but the essence of it all was, "What the . . . is going on? Why won't you answer me? Don't just sit there and look at me, do something!" I was confused and upset and angry. The only good news was that I didn't feel any pain.

Then I heard my name: "Howard, come here." And I wondered where this was coming from. There were different voices calling me from out of the doorway, and it was dim and hard to see. These voices said they were here to fix me up. "Come with us," they said. And I replied, "Well, who are you? Are you doctors and nurses?" And they said, "You'll see. Come on, quick, quick. You'll see, you'll find out." They kept evading my questions. They just seemed intent on getting me to step through the doorway. When I finally did, I was in a fog, a haze, and the people were hard to see, like silhouettes. It would be hard for me to describe them, because all I saw were murky figures. They kept saying, "Come on, hurry up." So I looked back into the room, and I saw my wife and Michel, and it was clear they couldn't help me, so I decided to follow these people. They led me through this haze.

I want to stress that there was a real sense of time-lessness in this entire experience. How long all this took is hard to say. But it felt like we walked and walked and walked, maybe even for days and weeks. And these peo-

ple were getting increasingly more aggressive about leading me along into this fog, which just kept getting thicker
and thicker. And it scared me a bit. I got to the point that
I didn't want to follow them anymore, but I didn't know
how to get back. So I just kept following them. I didn't
know where I was. I wasn't sure if I was alive or dead.
Then I told them I wouldn't go any further, so they started
to push and shove me, saying, "Oh yes you are."

About this time it became clear to me that I was an
amusement to these figures who were pushing me along;
that my pain was their pleasure. They weren't trying to
kill me, they were simply trying to make me hurt more.
Then they began clawing at me and biting at me. And just
as I'd get one off, it seemed as though five more would
be back on me, clawing and pushing. I had the sense that
there were innumerable numbers of these people clawing
at me, working to make me as miserable as possible.

It was essentially an atmosphere of darkness, fear, pain,
and utter loneliness. So at this point, I said to myself, Pray
to God. But I said, Hey, I don't pray. I don't do that. And
the voice inside once again said, Pray to God. So I went
like this: "The Lord is my shepherd, makes me walk
through the valley of the shadow of death . . ." Then these
creatures all around just went into a frenzy as I began to
utter these things, like I'd thrown them into boiling oil.
They began to scream at me, "Cut that out. What do you
think you are doing. You are such a coward, there is no
God, nobody can help you. We have no respect for you."
They were just screaming and yelling and swearing at me,
but they were also backing away from me as if I were
poison. So I kept on praying and calling out to God. This
went on for quite some time, until finally I realized I was
sitting there alone in the darkness. The little tormenters
had all gone away.

Sitting alone there in the darkness I felt this profound

sense of hopelessness, loneliness. I felt crippled, broken, and utterly alone. I didn't even have the strength to lift myself up onto my feet. I felt as though I was fading out, that I was sinking into the darkness. Then a most unusual thing happened. I heard something in my own voice that I remembered from Sunday School. I began to sing a little song, "Jesus loves me, Jesus loves . . ." And all of a sudden, and I don't know why, I really wanted to believe that. I wanted to cling to that.

Then I just screamed out into the darkness, "Jesus, please just save me." I screamed this out with everything I had, and then I saw, way off in the darkness, the tiniest little star, like a comet or a meteor, getting brighter and brighter, coming toward me like a rocket. Very bright. It started off as a speck of tiny light, but it just got brighter and brighter as it was rushing toward me. Finally, it came right up to me and its radiance was all around me and all through me. Then I rose up, not with my own effort, but by the force of the light. I just got lifted up off that place. And I saw this very, very plainly. I saw all my wounds, all my tears, all my brokenness just melt away, so that I became whole again in this great radiance.

I cried and cried and cried and cried. I was crying because I was feeling things I'd never felt before in my life. And I knew then that this radiance knew me, knew me better than my mother knows me, or my father knows me, my wife knows me. It conveyed to me that it loved me in a way that I can't begin to express, so I'm not even going to try to express that. I knew that this radiant being was powerful because it was making me feel so good all over; I could feel its light all over me. It was very gentle, and I felt it hold me and carry me up and out of the darkness, faster and faster and faster. And way off in the distance I saw something like the picture of a galaxy, a great center of brilliance. It was so powerful and so overwhelming that

I said, "Put me back, put me back." I was so ashamed of who I was that I wanted to be sent back into the monster pit. I just wanted to hide in the darkness. I didn't want to go toward the light anymore because I knew I didn't deserve it. I mean I did want the light, but I didn't, if you can understand that.

All of a sudden, for the first time, the light being next to me said, "You belong here." And I said, "No, put me back." And he said, "No, you belong here. We don't make mistakes." Then my light friend called out into the darkness and a number of brilliant illumined beings came to join us. I was still crying, and they said to me, "Are you afraid of us?" I said, "No." But they said, "We can turn this light down and appear to you as people." And I said, "No, don't do that. Please, don't do that, you are the most beautiful, wonderful things I've ever seen." I'm an artist, and here I was seeing a primary spectrum with at least eighty new colors. I was seeing this great brilliance, which is impossible to describe; colors, opalescence, beauty, not in any form I'd ever seen. What they were showing me was their glory.

Then they wanted to talk about my life. I saw my life play out before me, from beginning to end, very much in their control. And it was clear they were trying to teach me something, because they slowed down and zoomed in on specific moments and let other things run by more rapidly. It was more or less the whole show, although seen in a way that I'd never understood it before. All the things that I'd worked to achieve meant nothing to them. I could feel their feelings of sorrow and joy about various aspects of my life. They didn't look down on my achievements, mind you, they just didn't respond to them. What they responded to was how I'd interacted with other people. And unfortunately, most of my interactions with other people were pretty sad, pretty manipulative. The hypocrisy of my life was just nauseating. It all made me very sad, but the beings continued to radiate me with their love. And whenever the moments of my life were shown when I was truly loving, the beings felt great pleasure. Either way, they radiated great compassion to me, their love was tremendous.

Then the beings said, "Do you want to ask questions?" I had a million questions, and I asked them, but I'm not going to go into that now. Suffice it to say that the beings told me that the world was God's garden, and that the goal of life was to grow into an understanding of the Creator by shedding our egos, our shells, and reaching out to him. The only truly important work was to have a more intimate relationship with God.

I was never in heaven. I never saw God. I was up in the far, far suburbs, you might say, but it was full of beauty and love. I said, "I'm ready to be with you forever." But they said, "No, you must go back." And I said, "No, I can't. I don't want to go back." I tried to argue with them to let me stay. "If I go back," I said, "I'll become what I was before. I'll become a beast and an animal. So don't send me back." They said, "Do you think we expect you to be perfect? When you make a mistake, ask for forgiveness, and before you utter it you are forgiven, but you must ask for it. Try not to repeat mistakes. Learn, move on. The purpose of your life is to learn how to make your will God's will."

Well, then I shot back to my body. And to this day I've been wrestling with the implications of that experience. I even went on to seminary. Now I'm serving as a pastor at a United Church of Christ.

Hellish NDEs such as Storm's are rarely reported in our time, either because they really do occur infrequently or because people are reluctant to share them. In days gone by, however, experiences such as Storm's were reported far more often than they are today. Professor Carol Zaleski, a Harvard-trained medievalist, argues this persuasively in her scholarly study of NDEs, *Otherworld Journeys.* As she demonstrates, the most glaring difference between near-death stories drawn from the past and contemporary accounts is that experiencers in previous generations rarely ascended instantly to heaven. Instead, like Howard Storm, they were first forced to take an unpleasant journey through the underworld.

Professor Zaleski also notes that the majority of near-death experiencers in the past said they first had to undergo a series of trials or tests before they were accepted into heaven. Often, they spoke about crossing a barrier of some sort, most frequently a door, a gate, or a bridge protected by powerful guardian deities or beasts who were reluctant to let them enter. One of the most commonly cited barriers of entry into heaven was known as "the test bridge." "A bridge so narrow," as one medieval near-death experiencer put it, "that it could scarce take the width of one footstep." Good souls were said to be able to cross this narrow bridge with ease, and once on the other side they would presently be directed to heaven by an angel. Sinners, on the other hand, would plunge into the river of death below, to be tormented by devils.

Many people mistakenly believe that Christianity is alone in its portrayal of the after-death journey as an ordeal fraught with dangers. But this is far from true. The idea of hell has been depicted in Greek, Judaic, Moslem, and Egyptian literature, as well as in Hinduism and Buddhism. Hell, you might say, has a long and illustrious tradition the world over.

One of the earliest Western depictions of death as an ordeal is found in the five-thousand-year-old Egyptian Book of the Dead, an elaborate collection of prayers, incantations, and mythological tales about the afterlife. Here it is written that the newly deceased do not gain instant entrance into heaven. They must first journey to the dark underworld kingdom known as Tuat, the realm of the god Osiris. Tuat was divided into twelve regions, each of which could be entered only through a gate protected by three guardian deities. These guardians presented the newly deceased with a variety of specific dangers and challenges, among them blazing heat, deadly vapors, and a variety of terrifying beasts, such as the great sea serpent, Aapep, who repeatedly sought to devour the new arrivals.

Traversing the underworld valley of Tuat was challenging and frightening, but a necessary step for anyone who sought some measure of peace after death. For those who passed the initial tests, the final destination in Tuat was called the Sekhat Aru, or Field of Reeds. Here they would be forced to undergo judgment. Their hearts would be weighed in a scale against a feather, symbolizing the goddess of justice, Maat. If they failed the test, they would be eaten by the monster Amemet, a combination of crocodile, lion, and hippopotamus. If they passed the test, they would either be free to remain in the Field of Reeds with Osiris as their king, or, if they were a follower of the sun god, Amen Ra, to gain passage on his glorious solar barge, where they would journey pleasantly through a sea of light for the remainder of eternity.

In the Eastern traditions of Hinduism and Buddhism, similar mythologies of hell and judgment are found. In these traditions it is understood that we carry but two things with us into our deaths: our karma, which includes the sum total of all of our deeds, and the willfulness of our commitments. If we carry a tremendous amount of good karma with us into death, and our will had been directed primarily toward the highest spiritual goals, we are ensured either a happy rebirth or complete spiritual enlightenment. If, on the other hand, we carry a great deal of negative karma or a low level of spiritual willfulness into our deaths, we will initially be subjected to a variety of confrontations, either with beasts of prey or the raging forces of nature. Our deaths, in other words, would be filled with a tremendous sense of terror.

However, hell has never been viewed as a permanent place in Eastern mythologies. It is seen as a temporary learning station in the cycle of death and rebirth. With enough effort, even the most mean-spirited souls can eventually work themselves out of hell. But it would be deemed most unlikely that a morally bankrupt individual could achieve total spiritual liberation without first perfecting himself in an entire new round of lifetimes. The ascent to enlightenment would be long and hard—but it was never ruled out. In this sense, the religions of the East are based on an entirely optimistic theology. Spiritual enlightenment is within the realm of possibility for everyone. With enough time and effort, each of us has the capacity to wake up to spiritual truth, to "recognize ourselves," as one Hindu scholar put it, "as an integral part of a sacred interconnectedness."

In Judaism, Christianity, and Islam, hell has generally been viewed as a permanent place: once sent there, you were doomed for all eternity. This explains in part why there is such an emphasis in Western traditions on judgment and the necessity for moral righteousness in the here and now, because there are to be no second chances. It also explains why the concept of purgatory was eventually conceived in the Christian world, for it offered something of a proving ground, a halfway house, you might say, for those unfortunate souls who were neither so virtuous as to deserve the fruits of heaven, nor so evil as to deserve the torments of hell. It offered the spiritually undeveloped a chance to improve themselves before the final moment of judgment.

MAKING SENSE OF HELL

The point of this discussion is not to rekindle ancient fears of fire and brimstone but to emphasize that hell has long played a dominant role in the world's religious and mythological traditions. It therefore remains a concept deeply imbedded in human consciousness. Yet if this is so, then why are near-death stories such as Howard Storm's so very rare in our time? Is it because hell does not exist? Or is it due to other factors?

I think the first thing to note about Storm's NDE is that it was not entirely negative. Eventually, through the process of prayer and self-surrender, he said that he was able to escape the hellish realm and ascend to the light. Dr. Kenneth Ring has called experiences such as Storm's "inverted NDEs," because they occur in much the same manner as classic NDEs yet are perceived negatively by the experiencer. As Ring writes, such a "person reports all the usual events—having an out-of-body experience, going through a tunnel, encountering a light, and so on—but responds to these features from a standpoint of fear rather than peaceful acceptance." Storm obviously fits this mold. His NDE was pervaded by a tremendous sense of fear; a fear that intensified dramatically until he finally cried out for help.

Why was Howard Storm so filled with fear when the great majority of near-death experiencers today are not? According to near-death researchers Dr. Bruce Greyson and Nancy Evans Bush, the answer is obvious: "The person who responds this way is likely to be terrified by the prospect of losing one's ego in the process. As a result, the experience of dying is resisted strenuously rather than being surrendered to. It is this very resistance that creates the filter of increasing fear that comes to pervade the entire experience."

If Greyson and Bush are correct, Howard Storm's negative NDE makes perfect sense. He entered the dying process as a confirmed skeptic who believed that death was "a big zero, the big blackout." By his own admission, he was also an extremely self-centered and controlling person, not the sort of man who easily "surrendered" to anything, let alone the death process. Fearful of losing control of his life, of losing his ego, he fought the process of dying, which only served to escalate his fear.

Eight hundred years before the research of Greyson and Bush, the Tibetan Book of the Dead put forth a similar argument. In that book it is written that the thoughts, hopes, and fears we live with will be carried along with us into our deaths. The authors of the Tibetan Book of the Dead were convinced that those who die in a state of attachment to their ego, or in a state of fear, anger, or struggle, would undoubtedly undergo a hellish after-death journey. Those, on the other hand, who had prepared themselves to set aside their egos at death would come to recognize the universe as a single unified strand of unbroken wholeness to which they belonged forever. Thus delivered from the fear of annihilation, enlightened souls would meet the transition of death with gratitude and joy, emancipated at last to live forever with the infinite compassion of the Buddha.

The good news about most hellish experiences is that they eventually revert to classic NDEs. Storm described this process earlier when he said that the moment he began to pray, "these creatures all around just went into a frenzy." Eventually, after his continued prayer, they went away altogether, leaving him alone in the darkness. It was then that he screamed out, "Jesus, please just save me." The next thing he saw was a tiny speck of light far off in the distance. From that point on, his NDE reverted to the classic form.

Emanuel Swedenborg, one of the great religious visionaries of the eighteenth century, said that he underwent a hellish NDE similar to Storm's. He eventually came to conclude that "God never turns his face away from man, and never rejects man from himself. . . . He casts no one into hell and is angry with no one, the reason being that God is good himself, love itself, mercy itself. Consequently it is individuals . . . turning away from God." George Ritchie arrived at the same conclusion after returning from his hellish NDE. As he wrote in his book *Return from Tomorrow*, a hellish experience is easily avoided so long as we turn to the light: "Whether it was physical appetite, an earthly concern, an absorption with self—whatever got in the way of His light created the separation into which we stepped at death."

What saved Howard Storm? He was saved, he told me, because he finally cast aside his ego, his pride, and his vanity to reach out to the light. "What I learned from this experience is too powerful to deny: so long as we reach out to God, God is going to be there for us. To me, this is the undeniable law of spiritual life."

Is hell, then, simply the absence of light?

6

ENCOUNTERS WITH THE LIGHT OF GOD

God's body is light. . . .
—Zarathushtra, "Songs of Zarathushtra"

The seekers of the light are one.
—Samuel Longfellow,
"O Life That Maketh All Things New"

You are the light of the world.
—Jesus (Matthew 5:14)

The great majority of those near-death experiencers I spoke with were fortunate enough to bypass hell. After a brief moment of disorientation when they initially left their bodies, most of them headed directly for, as one experiencer called it, "the great brilliant white light that is God." Retired army sergeant John Wintek had this to say about his encounter with the light:

As soon as I saw the light, I began to struggle toward it. I wanted to go so badly because I knew it was God and I wanted to remain with him. . . . Sadly, I can tell you every detail of my experience, but I am unable to recapture the wonderful euphoric feeling which the presence of God provides.

While most of the near-death experiencers I spoke with were convinced that the light was God, I was often struck by the deep levels of frustration they felt in their efforts to describe the nature of this Divine Presence. Almost invariably, their interviews with me began in much the same manner as Wintek's, with an apology of some sort. "I'm so sorry," one experiencer told me, "it is just impossible for me to describe the beauty of what I saw." Another spoke for them all when he commented:

> Before my own experience, I thought I understood God. I knew there was no Old Man with a white beard. I had done quite a bit of reading of esoteric material and thought I had somewhat of an idea that God was bigger than the Old Man and was rather a "Force" of some sort.
> During my experience I realized that no matter how large a force I envisioned, it was still too limited to encompass God. I found that it is not possible to imagine God, and that it is okay to not know something, to be unable to define (and therefore limit) something.[1]

I think it is important to remember that when people talk about the nature of God, or the afterlife, they are trying to describe what cannot be described, in the only way available to them—in terms of the here and now. Like the many authors of the great sacred texts in religious history, those who have had near-death experiences are painfully aware that words, similes, and analogies simply cannot do justice to the nature of God. As most experiencers gladly admit, any of the many images of beauty and splendor they put forth are nothing more than an attempt to describe the unutterably magnificent.

In the history of religion, two schools of thought have emerged on what we can say about the nature of God. In Hinduism and Taoism it has long been stressed that God, or what followers of these traditions often prefer to call Ultimate Reality, is totally ineffable. In theological circles this has come to be called the *apophatic* tradition. Apophatic religions hold that in the face of God, silence is the only proper posture. This position was wonderfully expressed by the great Chinese sage Lao-tzu (approximately five hundred years before the birth of Christ) when he said that the Tao is "an undifferentiated yet perfect being, born before Heaven and Earth. . . . We may think of it as the Mother of this world, but I do not know its name; I shall call it Tao; were I forced to give it a name, it would be the immense." He went on to formulate the classic position of all apophatic faiths: "The Tao that can be told is not the eternal Tao. The name that can be named is not the eternal name."

Very shortly after Lao-tzu's death, the Buddha arrived at a similar conclusion, for he said exceedingly little to his followers about the nature of the Ultimate Reality he encountered in his peak moments. This is why, to this day, Buddhist teachers stress that the supreme teaching of their faith is not to be handed down by words but resides in the serene silence of the Buddha.

One of the most unusual apophatic approaches to comprehending the mystery of God was advanced by the Jewish philosopher Maimonides in the twelfth century. He said we could only talk about the nature of God when we focused on what God isn't, not on what God is. Maimonides' point was that no matter what we say about God, it is more likely to be false than true. His approach came to be called the *via negativa*, or the negative way, because he argued that the only way to talk about God was by way of negative statements. God is not this, God is not that. By categorizing all the things God was not, Maimonides believed we could eventually gain some insights into what God is.

The Christian religious tradition is decidedly *cataphatic*, since it has long held the belief that we can and must say something about our encounters with God. Still, Christian theologians generally stress that whatever we say about God is sure to miss the mark, that our attempts will at best be nothing more than gross approximations. As Saint John of Damascus once said, "God is above all essence." Despite our most valiant efforts, in other words, God simply cannot be fitted into our concepts or words. We are free to try, of course, so long as we recognize that our efforts are slated for failure.

Although Eastern religions have generally stressed silence when it comes to talking about God, we still find in them numerous corresponding references to the warm and brilliant light described by those who have had near-death experiences. In the Tibetan Book of the Dead, for example, it is said that shortly after death we initially enter into a dark or empty space. When we reawaken, however, we find ourselves bathed in the luminosity of a brilliant "clear light," which explains why that book opens with the following line: "To the Divine Body of Truth, The Incomprehensible, Boundless light . . ." In Hindu theology we are told that Brahma, or God, is identical with Atman, or the individual self, and that the entire phenomenal world, and every thing within it, is actually a manifestation of the Divine. Hence the insight of the great Indian sage Shankara: that the "Atman shines with its own light" for "this universe is nothing but Brahma."

Similar references to light are found in the religions of the West. In the Psalms, for example, we are told that God is "wrapped in the light like a cloak." In the New Testament, Jesus insisted that "we came from the light." He also said that "the kingdom of God is within you," intimating that while we live here on earth we can come to know this light so long as we recognize it within ourselves. In the Egyptian Book of the Dead it is said that the ultimate aim is to arrive at the light after death, which surely explains why the original Egyptian title for the book was *Pert em Hru*, which is best translated as "Coming Forth into the Light."

WHOSE GOD?

In the popular press, NDEs are generally reported because of the insights they offer us about an afterlife. Yet apart from insights we may gain about life after death from studying NDEs, they also provide us with something else quite significant: a collective vision of how humans see God. Do atheists and agnostics see God any differently than Hindus, Jews, or Christians? Here are a few examples of the ways near-death experiencers have attempted to describe their encounters with the light.

Christian experiencer Eleanor Tokash told me this:

When I arrived at the light, it encompassed me. I viewed it as Jesus, as God, for to me they are one and the same. It was comforting, everything I always expected or wanted or needed. It was the answer to everything. Glorious, magnificent. I met Jesus and God, and now I'll never be afraid to die. I know I'm going home.

Another Christian experiencer, Barbara Baird, had this to say:

[I saw] a cluster of stars, and this cluster was a very bright white light, and I wanted to count them, but I couldn't seem to do that. I did not sense that the stars were God, though, but they were my destination. The Divine Pres-

102

ence was not the stars. The Divine Presence was all around me, radiating such good feelings. I guess you might say that I felt the Divine Presence rather than saw it. How can I describe a feeling of being in the presence of God? All I know is that during my NDE I was in the heart of God, for I could see that God pervaded all matter, all being, all space, all non-space, everything. The Divine Presence was everywhere.

A Buddhist experiencer told me that he:

saw the great white light, and it was brilliant. It was what we call Shunyata, or total emptiness. In this emptiness— which is not a fearful thing, but a marvelous thing—there was peace, calm, a sense of being freed from the ego. I didn't achieve enlightenment, but I got a taste of what it might be like.

Another person who had an NDE said:

It was just pure consciousness. And this enormously bright light seemed almost to cradle me. I just seemed to exist in it and be part of it and be nurtured by it and the feeling just became more and more ecstatic and glorious and perfect.[2]

As these examples show, the light of the NDE has been identified in numerous ways. Some experiencers have called it Jesus. Others have called it a "presence," or a "light being." Others call it "pure consciousness." Still others simply call it "God." A Buddhist experiencer identified the light as Shunyata, or emptiness, which is rightly understood as the ultimate goal of Buddhism.

There has been a great deal of speculation as to why nearly every near-death experiencer talks about an encounter with the light yet identifies it in so many different ways. In other words, while the light appears to be a universal and invariable aspect of NDEs, identifications of it do not. Why is this so?

In my view, there is only one logical explanation: while the light is indeed universal and invariable in NDEs, we each bring to it our own set of cultural, religious, and personal expectations. As the rabbis of the Midrash told us, "God is like a mirror. The mirror never changes but everyone who looks at it sees a different face." More simply put, the experience of light is conditioned by one's life experiences. Buddhist teacher and author Sogyal Rinpoche makes this point nicely in *The Tibetan Book of Living and Dying*. According to him, the deities we see in our NDEs are

> not unique to Tibetans; they are a universal and fundamental experience, but the way they are perceived depends on our conditioning. Since they are by nature limitless, they have the freedom then to manifest in any form . . . therefore the deities can take on the forms we are most familiar with in our lives. For example, for Christian practitioners, the deities might take the form of Christ or the Virgin Mary. Generally, the whole purpose of the enlightened manifestation of the Buddha (for Buddhist practitioners) is to help us, so they may take on whatever form is most appropriate and beneficial to us. But in whatever form the deities appear, it is important to recognize that there is definitely no difference whatsoever in their fundamental nature.

So the way we have thought, lived, and believed in our lives will likely determine the way we identify the light at the time of our deaths—and near-deaths. If we are prepared to meet the Buddha, or Christ, or Shiva, that is what we will call what we encounter. If we are not prepared to meet such figures, we will simply see a brilliant light. Either way, from all descriptions, this divine encounter is certain to fill us with great peace, warmth, and joy.

AN ENCOUNTER, NOT AN EXPERIENCE

After meeting with a wide variety of near-death experiencers, I find it difficult to escape the conclusion that these meetings with the light of God are a great deal more profound than simple *experiences*. Rather, they are *encounters* of the highest order. This is why the term NDE troubles me somewhat, because the word *experience* fails to adequately convey the potency of these rare exchanges between men and women and their God. Martin Buber, the great twentieth-century Jewish philosopher, addressed this problem in his spiritual classic *I and Thou* when he stressed that "experiences" are very often nothing more than one-way events in which the observer experiences something while the observed does not. The observed is passive, unaffected, unengaged. The word *encounter*, on the other hand, suggests a meeting of minds and hearts, a sense of sharing, in which both parties come away touched and affected by the engagement.

The encounter with the light of God described by near-death experiencers is one of intimate mutuality; they encounter God, but God also encounters them. The relationship appears to be one of give and take. As one experiencer explained, "It's something which becomes you and you become it. I could say, 'I was peace, I was love.' I was the brightness, it was part of me. . . ." Another person recalled, "This enormously bright light seemed almost to cradle me. I just seemed to exist in it and be part of it and be nurtured by it, and the feeling just became more and more ecstatic and glorious and perfect." Truly deep encounters, truly fulfilling connections between people, nature, and God, have a way of evoking such positive feelings.

THE GIFTS OF LIGHT

What does the light give near-death experiencers in this mutual encounter? According to the men and women I have met, there appear to be seven principle gifts. These are: (1) freedom from physical suffering; (2) reassurance about the existence of God; (3) faith in the reality of life after death; (4) a powerful sense of the unity of life; (5) gratitude and joy; (6) the opportunity for life review; and, finally, (7) spiritual transformation. These last two gifts have such far-reaching spiritual and psychological implications that I will devote a separate chapter to each of them.

FREEDOM FROM PHYSICAL SUFFERING

Since most near-death experiencers arrive at the light after undergoing great physical trauma of one sort or another, they are especially thankful for the gift of freedom from physical suffering. Although it is a simple gift, it is hugely appreciated. As one person who had an NDE told me:

I went into the light, and my pain ceased completely. I was overjoyed, because up until that point I was suffering from some of the worst pain imaginable. My pain was so great that I wasn't even sure I could carry on. And I guess I didn't, because it was at this point that I entered the light. Words can't describe how thankful I was to be freed from all that pain.

Yet another experiencer, June Collins, told me:

> The doctor told me to breathe deeply and to cough to relieve my pain, but that only made things worse, so I cried out to the nurse to find something to help me, but she wasn't successful. The minute I left my body, however, the pain just went away. Suddenly I felt young and healthy and wonderful. I never felt so good in all my life. I had a terrible weight taken off of me. I felt so relieved, so thankful.

REASSURANCE ABOUT GOD'S EXISTENCE

As a result of their NDEs, most people are convinced that the one reality to which all of us ultimately belong is the light of God. To date, I have not met, heard, or read about a single person who has had a near-death experience who has not come away from his or her experience convinced that God, or some form of ultimate, transcendent reality, exists. As near-death experiencer John Wintek told me:

> Though I can remember today every detail of the experience as vividly as I did when I woke up in the hospital eleven years ago, the real value of the experience is in the fact that I encountered God. I came away from the experience with a profound sense of love and acceptance that colors my thinking and has given me an intense appreciation for my world and the people that inhabit it with me. . . . As for faith, it is no longer a matter of believing in or having faith in the existence of God and heaven. I know both God and heaven exist because I have been there and have seen the light of God's presence.

Another experiencer told me:

> I already believed in God prior to my experience. So my NDE just reinforced my belief in God, intensified it, because you cannot possibly find yourself within the light of that perfect love and not come away believing in your Creator. That's what you see in an NDE, you know, all the powers of creation, and yourself as a part of it all. When I felt all this love, and experienced myself wrapped in the light of creation, how could I not believe in God?

FAITH IN THE REALITY OF LIFE AFTER DEATH

Many told me that prior to their NDEs they thought they believed in life after death but that it wasn't until they actually encountered the light that their belief was transformed into an unwavering conviction. If there is one thing near-death experiencers are adamant about, it is this: death is not an end. As experiencer Elaine Durham told me:

> Before I died, I believed in a heavenly realm, but I didn't believe you could die and actually come back again. That is what astonished me. Now I know for certain that there is life after death. I also know that there are many other realms beyond this earthly one.

Another experiencer said:

> And as for the skeptics: going through an experience like that, afterward it just puts a belief into you that no matter what anybody says or whoever tries to disqualify these, it will never hold up with me because I believe I have seen something of where I'm eventually going.[3]

A POWERFUL SENSE OF THE UNITY OF LIFE

The encounter with divine light provides near-death experiencers with a great many pleasurable sensations, among them feelings of tremendous warmth and comfort. It also appears to provide them with a new and special form of knowledge, for most near-death experiencers will tell you that, in the process of beholding the divine light, they came to know—albeit momentarily—something of what God knows. As one experiencer expressed it, "As I became one with this omnipresent light, its knowledge became my knowledge." A British near-death experiencer said this:

What I did have was a complete and extensive knowledge, to the extent of being able to comprehend the purpose of life and Creation, because I was part of it, as when the body uses the ability to see, smell, taste and touch, hear, without prior knowledge.

What is this knowledge that the light imparts to those who have had near-death experiences? It is the knowledge that everything in the universe is ultimately connected together through divine love. As Emerson wrote, "We live in secession, in division, in parts, in particles. Meantime within man is the soul of the whole; the wise silence; the universal beauty, to which every part and particle is equally related; the eternal ONE." This same unitive understanding of life was captured nicely by someone I interviewed in Chicago who underwent a near-death experience:

When you see the light, it is as though it absorbs you, and somehow you become one with it. The light becomes you and you become the light. Which is not to say that I became God, but that God was happy to become me, if that makes any sense to you. I was never told by the light that

109

everything is connected or anything like that, because I didn't need to be told. I mean you just know it. All I was left with was an overwhelming, overflowing sense of joy and love.

Diana Schmidt, who underwent a clinical NDE in 1975 as a result of a powerful seizure that took hold of her while she was a patient in a California hospital, wrote to tell me this:

I was the light. I knew that future and past were all now. The now was the result of the oneness, and the oneness was the result of the absence of barriers. In the oneness I knew that I was pure, finally clean, and free because the oneness does not judge. I was also aware of everything, because I became everything.

Another experiencer said this:

There was no separateness at all. The peace that I felt was indescribable, it was something I have never known before and I have never been able to reach again. . . . I felt tremendous peace and oneness, the unity was indescribable.[4]

These quotes show that near-death experiencers are gifted with a momentary knowledge and understanding of a larger pattern of life, a comprehensive vision of the unity of creation that radically transcends normal human consciousness. History brims with similar descriptions of this expanded sense of awareness. In the Middle Ages, for example, Gregory the Great attributes the following unifying vision to Saint Benedict:

O abounding grace, by which I dared to fix my look on the Eternal Light so long that I spent all my sight upon it! In its depth I saw that it contained, bound by love in one volume, that which is scattered in the leaves through the universe, substances and accidents and their relations as it were fused together in such a way that what I tell of is simple light. I think I saw the universal form of this complex, because in telling of it I feel my joy expand.[5]

Dante said that those who encounter the light somehow "fuse" with the Divine. In the sixteenth century, the writer François-Louis de Blois captured the essence of this fusing with the Divine, and the special knowledge it imparts, in this description of his own experience:

Through the brilliancy of the divine light shining on my mind, it [the soul] loses all consideration and distinction of things and lays aside them all, even the most excellent images; and all liquefied by love, and, as it were, reduced to nothing, it melts away into God. It is then united to God without any medium, and becomes one spirit with Him, as iron placed in the fire is changed into fire, without ceasing to be iron.... Here the soul reposes ... sweetly experiencing the operation of God, it abounds with ineffable peace and joy.

GRATITUDE AND JOY

As the quotes in this chapter show, the encounter with light convinces near-death experiencers that God exists, that there is eternal life, and that the universe is finally unified and animated by a love so powerful and compassionate that the most aroused of human loves is pale by comparison. The great problems of existence momentarily vanish for near-death experiencers, so much so that they want to cry out, as one experiencer told me he did, "Yes! Yes! Now I understand! This is it! I am home!" The end result is expressed by near-death experiencers like John Wintek with profound feelings of gratitude and joy: "I saw a bright, glowing, pulsating light. I felt as one with it. I felt complete unification . . . no alienation whatsoever. The serenity and peace were nearly overwhelming . . . an intense feeling of love and joy."

What most of us secretly long for suddenly becomes a reality for those who have had near-death experiences: for a brief moment in time, they come to know—not just as any abstract intellectual concept, but as a palpable fact close to their hearts—that they belong to God. Thus charged, they awaken to the fact that both life and death are gifts.

7

THE FILM OF YOUR LIFE

∞

One day, when you return to the invisible world, you will
be examined on how you have applied the law of love. . . .
You will find yourself confronted by the film of your earthly
life, you will see the smallest details and notice the tiniest
errors and you will have to reform yourself. You must therefore reflect and concentrate on what you are saying and how
you are saying it. Here, you are an actor on stage, being
photographed and recorded for all time.

—Peter Deunov

The universal law of karma . . . is that of action and reaction,
cause and effect, sowing and reaping. In the course of natural
righteousness, man, by his thoughts and actions, becomes the
arbiter of his destiny.

—Paramahansa Yogananda

Do not judge, and you will not be judged; do not condemn,
and you will not be condemned. Forgive, and you will be
forgiven.

—Jesus (Luke: 6:37)

Each year a few weeks before Christmas, millions of young
children across America are introduced to the concept of the
life review, because one of the major television networks

113

will surely present some film version of Charles Dickens's famous tale about sad old Mr. Scrooge, *A Christmas Carol.* This past Christmas, my five-year-old son and I watched Walt Disney's cartoon version, which resulted in a number of discussions between us on the nature of "good guys and bad guys." In the story, Scrooge is an evil man who is taken from his bed one night by three ghosts who force him to review the most unsavory aspects of his life as a coldhearted penny-pincher. Through this life-review process, Scrooge comes to see that he has made an awful mess of his life and is given one last opportunity to reform himself, which he gratefully accepts.

In every significant way, the life-review process described by near-death experiencers is identical to the one Scrooge goes through. In the presence of the light, near-death experiencers are given the opportunity to review their lives, to reassess them, and to relive both the positive and negative consequences of their actions in an atmosphere of loving acceptance. They are also given the chance to reform themselves upon their return.

The contemporary British author and philosopher David Lorimer finds that there are essentially two sorts of life-review processes: the panoramic memory, and the life-review proper. Panoramic memories are defined by Lorimer as "a display of images and memories with little or no direct emotional involvement." The prevalent features of this experience are a sense of reality, vividness, and the accuracy of the images flashing rapidly before one's mind. Richard Todd, a New Yorker who has had a near-death experience, described his panoramic memory to me this way:

My entire life appeared before me in a moving motion picture at tremendous speed. I saw each and every significant milestone of my life whip by with total precision.

It was like I was watching a movie, just passively sitting there watching the drama of my life run by.

Although quite similar to the panoramic-memory experience just described, a full-blown life review has, in Lorimer's words, "the additional element of emotional involvement and a degree of moral assessment of the consequences of thoughts, feelings and actions." A good example of this more extensive life-review process is detailed by a person in Raymond Moody's book Reflections on *Life After Life*:

> The light was showing me what was wrong, what I did wrong. And it was very real.
> It seemed like this flashback, or memory ... was directed primarily at ascertaining the extent of my life. It was like there was a judgment being made and then, all of a sudden, the light became dimmer, and there was a conversation, not in words, but in thoughts. When I would see something, when I would experience a past event, it was like I was seeing it through eyes with (I guess you would say) omnipotent knowledge, guiding me, and helping me to see.
> That's the part that has stuck with me, because it showed me not only what I had done but even how what I had done had affected other people. And it wasn't like I was looking at a movie projector because I could feel these things; there was feeling, and particularly since I was with this knowledge. ... I found out that not even your thoughts are lost. ... Every thought was there. ... Your thoughts are not lost.[1]

This quote illustrates well the full-blown life-review process in that it shows how experiencers actually come to comprehend the consequences of their actions. Rather than standing dispassionately apart from the images as they would in a panoramic-memory experience, they become involved with the images, feel the images, and actually stand in judgment of themselves. I believe this is why so many near-death experiencers told me that "it wasn't really God who judged me; God just gave me an opportunity to judge myself."

THE OVERSOUL

Drawing his inspiration from the idealistic writings of Plato, Ralph Waldo Emerson believed that each of us, at heart, is "part and parcel of the Divine." In his famous essay on the subject, "The Oversoul," Emerson wrote about the divine nature that resides within us.[2] He was convinced that spiritual growth hinged almost entirely upon our ability to rediscover this oversoul within ourselves.

One of the most fascinating features of the NDE generally, and the life-review process in particular, is that it appears as if something very much like this oversoul emerges powerfully within experiencers, because they appear to achieve a widened sense of mental and emotional acuity that far transcends ordinary human consciousness. Experiencers not only obtain a more universal and impersonal viewpoint of their lives (a bird's-eye view, you might say), but also an enormous degree of empathy and compassion, not only for themselves but for all creation. "My consciousness seemed to expand beyond the limitations and confines of my brain," said Janice Cameron, a person from Minnesota who had a near-death experience. "I could see further, I could feel more intensely, I could hear better, and I felt the connections and relationships between things like never before."

Some, like Phyllis Atwater, say they expand in consciousness so greatly during their NDEs that they can even feel the influences of their actions on plants and animals:

> For me it was a total reliving of every thought I had ever thought, every word I had ever spoken, and every deed I had ever done; plus the effect of each thought, word, and deed on everyone who had ever come within my environment or sphere of influence whether I knew them or not (including unknown passersby on the street); plus the effect of each thought, word and deed on weather, plants, animals, soil, trees, water, and air.[3]

This powerful expansion of awareness appears to enable them to stand in judgment of themselves. Now, instead of viewing the world from the standpoint of their isolated egos, they acquire the ability—through the emergence of their oversoul—to view the larger tapestry of life, to grow beyond the smaller concerns and limitations of ordinary human consciousness.

David Lorimer calls this special ability "empathic resonance," because near-death experiencers expand so greatly in knowledge and empathy that they are able to see the world as an interconnected web to which they are inextricably bound. It is this recognition of their connectedness to creation that reminds them that they are responsible for far more than themselves. They see that if they hurt or injure others, they are actually doing harm to their greater self, because they are bound to every aspect of creation through "a sacred interconnectedness."

THE COMPASSIONATE COMPANION

While near-death experiencers ultimately judge themselves in the life-review process, they are seldom alone. Most told me they were joined by a "being of light" who is able, as one near-death experiencer put it, "to see right through me and reveal my deepest secrets." Often the being of light talks with those who have had near-death experiences, asking them a few simple questions, the most common being, "What do you have to show me of your life?" One woman said that it was God who addressed her:

> Instantly my entire life was laid bare and open to this wonderful presence, "God." I felt inside my being his forgiveness for the things in my life I was ashamed of, as though they were not of great importance. I was asked— but there were no words; it was straight mental instantaneous communication—"What had I done to benefit or advance the human race?" At the same time all my life was presented instantly in front of me and I was shown or made to understand what counted. I am not going into this any further but, believe me, what I had counted in life as unimportant was my salvation and what I thought was important was nil.[4]

I have not met a single person who has had a near-death experience who has not stressed that this questioning of deeds and motives is never carried out with malice, but with love, compassion, and immense understanding. If anything, the being of light appears not so much to judge near-death experiencers, but to help comfort them as they review the many painful and less savory moments of their lives, to help them in the process of forgiving themselves for their less than saintly behavior.

Here is what a person from Canton, Ohio, who has had a near-death experience, told me:

> The being of light radiated deep compassion to me, showing me the good and the ugly moments of my life without

passing judgment upon me. I felt respected, loved, cared for. Even when I stared at the worst moments of my life, I knew I had nothing to fear. The light being somehow helped me to find the courage to forgive myself for occasionally acting so selfishly, so self-centeredly. It was clear to me that this was all taking place to help me grow into a better person, and that took away a lot of the pain.

ULTIMATE LESSONS

Most of the near-death experiencers I spoke with told me that the primary purpose of the life review was to help them recognize that love alone is what matters. One experiencer put it simply, "All through this, he kept stressing the importance of love." Another, Keith Keller, who lives in Topeka, Kansas, told me:

> I know, it is an old cliché: love makes the world go round. But you know, that is true, don't you see that? I learned in my NDE that it is God's love that makes the world go round, and the more we lend our hand to God by loving others, as well as ourselves, the more we grow spiritually. The problem is that most of us just don't know how to love, do we? We are full of pride, jealousy, lust, and an almost insatiable craving for money and power. TV is full of this garbage. Why this is I don't know, but we are going to have to pay for this self-centered and unloving behavior one way or another, whether in this life or the next one. I think we pay for it now, though, right here on earth, because if you don't know how to love, you can't experience the joy of living. This is what my NDE taught me.

Another lesson that emerges is that "we reap what we sow," that the law of karma is operating relentlessly for everyone.

Those who have had near-death experiences come to understand that any harm they produce in this life will have to be relived and intensely felt at a later date. They cannot escape the consequences of their deeds. Personal responsibility for their actions must be accepted. This requires that they use tremendous care and purity of motive with regard to their thoughts, feelings, and actions. As the late Norman Cousins once cautioned us, "everything is of consequence."

RELUCTANCE TO RETURN

Because NDEs are generally quite positive, it is easy to understand why many of those I spoke with said that they had been tremendously reluctant to return to their bodies. Convinced they had finally come home to God, most wanted nothing more than to remain in the presence of the light. Carol Purcell, a woman from Florida who has had a near-death experience, who suffers from a rare form of lupus, spoke for many when she told me:

Why would anyone want to leave the company of God? I mean, here you are, perhaps for the first time in your life, feeling good about yourself—and loved by your Creator as you've never been loved before. That's why when I was told I was going to have to go back, I screamed, "Oh, no, please don't send me back. I want to stay with you." I was really angry, you know, because I couldn't understand why I had to go back. The next thing I knew I was back in the hospital, back in my body, and full of pain. I was very let down.

The intensity of this reluctance to return among near-death experiencers occasionally manifests itself in rude and defiant behavior. A case in point is Andy Petro, who managed to surprise himself when he confronted the light in his NDE:

> The only time I spoke to the light [in my NDE] was after I got this tremendous infusion of knowledge and joy. It was then that the light said to me, "Andy, you have to go back." And I said, "No I'm not." And it startled me, because for the first time in my life I became assertive. I mean, here I am, speaking to God, and I had never before even said no to my father. Here I am saying no to God. And the light said to me a second time, "Andy, you are going back." And again I said, "No, I'm not. I want to stay here." Finally, the third time the light said to me, "Andy, you are going back," I shot back into my body.

Responses such as Andy's are common in the history of near-death testimony. One example is found in the sixteenth-century NDE of Salvius. When told by the light that he must return to his body, he cried out, "Alas, alas, Lord, why have you shown me these things, if I was to be cheated of them?" Tundal, a twelfth-century man who had a near-death experience, responded similarly. He reported that during his NDE he was guided by an angel through an especially difficult life-review process that eventually culminated in an encounter with the light. When he asked his angel if he could stay, he was told that he did not yet deserve to remain in heaven. Upon hearing this unpleasant news, he cried out, "Lord, what great evils have I ever done that I must go back to my body, leaving such glory behind?" At this point Tundal's angel simply told him to remember all that he had seen in the afterlife and to be mindful of his behavior upon his return. He was then instantly sent back.

The great majority of near-death experiencers I interviewed responded in much the same manner as Andy Petro,

Salvius, and Tundal. Few wanted to leave the light, and many told me they vigorously protested being forced to return to their bodies. The only exceptions were the many mothers I interviewed, most of whom told me they put up much less of a struggle because they were convinced that their duties on earth required them to return. Cecilia Whalen, whose 1970 NDE was brought on by a severe case of meningitis, refused to die. Her two teenage children were going through difficult times, and she was intent on saving them. Here is what she told me:

> I remember the light was coming toward me, and I kept saying, "I don't want to die, I don't want to die." When I approached the light, it said, "What do you want?" I said, "I don't want to die. I want to go back. I want to save my children." And the light said to me again, "What do you want to do?" I said, "I want to save my children." It then said to me, "As long as you take care of the children, you're always going to be taken care of. But if you don't take care of the children, you will suffer." I said, "Yes, I understand,"and then I shot back to my body.

COMING BACK

Given the tremendous power of NDEs, it isn't surprising that the return to life requires considerable psychological and spiritual readjustment.

Many told me that one of the major issues they face upon their return is to decide whether or not to share their story with others. Will they be branded as lunatics or religious fanatics by their friends, neighbors, coworkers, and acquaintances? One experiencer, who prefers to remain unidentified, confided in me that "it took fifteen years before I shared the details of my experience with anyone. And you are maybe only the third person I've talked to. People tend to think you're a loony from the *Twilight Zone* if you say you had an NDE; they think you're nutty. I decided it was better to keep silent."

Bottling up the truth of what they went through is one of the many challenges near-death experiencers face, which may explain why near-death support groups have had such tremendous success in recent years. It is easier for experiencers to share their stories and insights in an atmosphere where they will be understood and accepted, and not questioned or ridiculed.

Another problem commonly reported by near-death experiencers is that they initially find it difficult to cope with the emotional effect of having seen a better world and having to live in this one. For some, this side effect has long-term consequences. One of the best examples of this was expressed by the novelist Katherine Anne Porter, who underwent an NDE in 1918 after a bout with influenza. As she said in an interview:

> I had seen my heavenly vision and the world was pretty dull after that. My mood for several years thereafter was that it was not a world worth living in. And yet one has faith, one has the inner core of strength that comes from somewhere, probably inherited from someone. Throughout my life there have been times during the day when I have both an intense wish to die and later an eagerness that can't wait to see the next day.

This quote nicely illustrates the truth that everything that goes up must eventually come down with a heavy thud. It also shows that while an NDE is an encounter with light, it does not necessarily lead to instant enlightenment. As we all know, it is one thing to see and experience the truth, quite another to live that truth in daily life.

Fortunately, the majority of near-death experiencers I spoke with found that after the initial shock of returning to their bodies, and after a brief period of readjustment, their lives dramatically changed for the better. Many reported to me a wide variety of positive personal transformations. Perhaps most significantly, near-death experiencers appear to return convinced that while God wills the ultimate destiny of the human race, the destiny of their lives lies entirely in their own hands: to succeed or fail, hate or love, create or destroy, within their own unique set of opportunities and circumstances. Now they have a job to do and the mission is clear: Will they strive mightily to live a life devoted to love, goodness, beauty, and truth? Or will they sink comfortably into the selfish materialism that mars the lives of so many of their fellow travelers on earth? The choice is theirs, and theirs alone, but now they see how careful they must be, for their very souls are at stake.

8

A NEW FAITH, A NEW LIFE

∞

One good deed is worth a thousand prayers.

—Zarathushtra

While the encounter with light does not provide near-death experiencers with instantaneous enlightenment, it nearly always transforms their outlook and behavior—usually for the better. As Andy Petro explained to me:

> If there was some way to do a psychological profile of me before and after my experience, there would be two different people, two very different personalities. I lost my fear as a result of my experience. I lost my sense of being worthless. I came back with a great sense of self-worth, self-love, and a tremendous amount of faith. Now I love people, I love being alive, and I'm having fun being alive, with all its pluses and minuses.

What happened to Andy also happened to most of the near-death experiencers with whom I spoke. They returned from their brushes with death with a powerful new faith; a faith that spawned a loss of worry and a vigorous sense of assurance in their lives, along with a far greater degree of inner peace and tranquility. This new faith also instilled in them a conviction that the mysteries of life now finally made sense, and promoted a spiritual and psychological renewal process that invariably instilled new meaning and purpose in their lives.

Dr. Raymond Moody was understandably fascinated by the many personal transformations that occur in people in the aftermath of NDEs. Back in the mid-seventies, when he first wrote about the subject, he isolated eight principle changes that emerge in the lives of those who have had near-death experiences. Expanding on Moody's work, Dr. Kenneth Ring studied the many "value shifts" that ensue in experiencers' lives. The greatest change noted by Moody and Ring was that near-death experiencers appear to shift from an outward, materialistically oriented philosophy of life to an inward, spiritually directed quest for meaning.

My own interviews with near-death experiencers certainly confirm the findings of Moody and Ring, but I have managed to derive a set of ten principle changes brought about by NDEs. Three of these changes I have already discussed in earlier chapters: namely, an unwavering faith in the existence of God or some ultimate force; a faith that there is some form of life after death and that this life beyond is enormously pleasant; and, finally, a faith that, as the noted psychologist Abraham Maslow phrased it, "the whole universe is ... an integrated and unified whole ... that the universe is all of a piece and that one has one's place in it— one is part of it, one belongs to it."

It is significant to note that in his pioneering work on "peak experiences," Dr. Maslow repeatedly stressed that these gifts of faith are often so profound that they "change a person's character and *Weltanschauung* [worldview] forever after." The remainder of this chapter is devoted to the seven additional ways in which NDEs tend to alter the spiritual worldview and behavior of experiencers. Before I begin, however, I wish to stress that not all of those who have had near-death experiences are transformed in each of these seven ways. As I said before, NDEs are not a ticket to instantaneous enlightenment. A few of the experiencers I spoke with were not as deeply impacted by their NDEs as the others. Yet, as I believe the following quotes will show, generally NDEs are tremendously positive, life-transforming experiences that call people to live their lives with a vastly heightened sense of purpose.

A Potent Desire to Live in the Present

One of the most dramatic changes that occurs in the lives of near-death experiencers is that their concern for the past and future diminish markedly. The concept of time (like the concept of death) becomes utterly irrelevant to most of them. "Time is nonexistent because everything is eternal. But most people don't see this. That's why they so often confuse change with death. But death is impossible," explains Lynn Pielage-Kissel, a woman who had a near-death experience and is now a Buddhist. "My experience taught me that the only thing that matters is the present, because if we can leave behind our regrets over the past, or fears for the future, we can awaken more easily to the beauty of what is in front of us each moment. Living in the present is what I'm after now, not some far-off goal in the future."

Convinced as they are that time has little or no meaning, most near-death experiencers seem to agree that an important aim in life is to learn how to accept and grow with change in a gracious, loving, and immensely appreciative manner: the goal is to wake up to the gift of what one experiencer I met calls the "precious present." As so many of them told me, the crucial thing is to extract the most meaning from each and every drop of life. Poet and mystic

William Blake captured the essence of this outlook in his enchanting poem, "Eternity."

> He who binds to himself a joy
> Does the winged life destroy.
> But he who kisses the joy as it flies
> Lives in eternity's sun rise.

The majority of near-death experiencers would agree with Blake that life is to be lived in the moment and appreciated for what it is, rather than for what we wish it might be. Time and again, near-death experiencers have told me that life is to be lived in a state of acceptance, surprise, and immense gratitude. "The first thing I saw when I awoke in the hospital was a flower, and I cried," said one woman who had had a near-death experience. "Believe it or not, I had never really *seen* a flower until I came back from death." Another, Barbara Baird, told me:

After my NDE I came to appreciate the present much more, because this is really all we have, you know. But this didn't happen immediately. It was something that developed within me over time. It happened without me really realizing it, too. All I know is that now I realize that every single day that I live, every little moment, is precious. My NDE gave this to me.

You know, sometimes I get a little cranky with people who don't understand this; people who don't see how really beautiful life is. People who get angry over little inconsequential things sometimes bring me to the brink of upset. Like people who get angry over being cut off in traffic, or something so silly as that. When this happens I just try to remind myself that I have been somewhere they haven't been. I've been on the other side and I have learned that we have nothing to fear. I have learned that love alone is what is important. It saddens me that so many people just don't yet realize how crazy it is to waste time getting angry over things that are so insignificant.

A NEW FEELING OF CONTROL AND SELF-CONFIDENCE

"One thing I noticed when I came back from my NDE was that I gained a new sense of confidence," a young man told me. He continued:

An example occurred recently when we had some trouble in our church. I remember there was great confusion over what we were going to do to solve the problem, but I could see very clearly the right path to go as a result of my NDE. And I wasn't at all afraid to voice this to the congregation. Before my NDE I probably wouldn't have done this. I'd have sat it out. It seems I've developed a calm at my core, a calm inside me. And when things get confused and wild, all I do is step back for a moment and tap into this core of calmness. When I do, I find that all of my decisions are more centered and better.

These feelings are not unusual. In the near-death support groups I've attended, I was often struck by the certitude and confidence exhibited by experiencers. Perhaps the presence of supportive friends encourages such confidence, but still NDEs generally wipe away the fear of death, which appears to free experiencers up to live more decisively. Convinced, with Thoreau, that "Your religion is where your love is," near-death experiencers often want nothing else but to bring more love into the world. And this requires confidence, self-assertiveness, and an unwavering conviction that one's actions can have a significant impact on the destiny of humankind.

A DECREASED INTEREST IN MATERIAL VALUES

In his exhaustive statistical study of NDEs, *Heading Toward Omega*, Dr. Kenneth Ring collected a large sampling of questionnaires from near-death experiencers focusing on the value changes that occurred in their lives. One thing this rich body of statistical data illustrates is that NDEs greatly weaken people's commitment to the superficial values of wealth, achievement, and fame. Dr. Stanislav Grof, who has done a tremendous amount of research in the area of altered states of consciousness, believes this decreased interest in materialistic values can be attributed to the fact that near-death experiencers come to accept change and impermanence as the only constants in life. This in turn appears to awaken in them a realization, as he writes, "of the absurdity and futility of exaggerated ambitions, attachment to money, status, fame, and power, or pursuit of other temporal values."

My own work with near-death experiencers corroborates Grof's insight. Let us now look at a few accounts in which this attitude toward life is described.

I still like to look nice and dress nice, but that is not really important. New cars and furniture and things like that just aren't important at all. I don't care about what other people think anymore, either, and I don't care about fashion. As far as the house is concerned, I like it to look pretty and clean, but it is more important to me that people feel they can come into my home and feel welcome and safe. As far as my car is concerned, it just helps me get from place to place. As long as it runs, as long as I can get in and out of it, why, that is all right.

I realized that there are things that every person is sent to earth to realize and to learn. For instance, to share more love, to be more loving toward one another. To discover that the most important thing is human relationships and love and not materialistic things. And to realize that every single thing that you do in your life is recorded and that even though you pass it by, not thinking, at the time, it always comes up later.[1]

Before my NDE I was already on the spiritual path. I was a missionary, and I set up a community free-meals program through my church, so I can't say that I was totally changed by the experience. What I can say is that it confirmed, clarified, and intensified much of what I already believed. For example, as much as I like things, material things, we always buy used cars. Because I don't feel it necessary to make a statement through what I own. My husband is a successful attorney, and we could live a lot more lavishly than we do, but we don't feel any need— or desire. I've always ascribed to the less-is-more philosophy of life, and my NDE just confirmed this very simple, spiritual approach to life.

A SPIRITUAL AS OPPOSED TO RELIGIOUS ORIENTATION

Several years ago I met an Orthodox rabbi who was terribly funny and immensely human. We were conversing on the subject of religion in a kosher deli in St. Paul, Minnesota. He told me that one of his greatest frustrations as a rabbi was that far too many of his congregants were caught up in the trappings of religion rather than the practice of spirituality, which for him meant taking the time to listen to God. "When God came down to Mount Sinai," he told me animatedly, "the one thing he asked us to do was to not go religious on him. When God came and wanted to talk to us, the first thing he had to say was, 'Cut that out. Stop it with this religion already and listen to me.'"

Most of the near-death experiencers I met would readily agree with the sentiments expressed by this rabbi. "God couldn't care less about religion," exclaimed one woman. An Australian near-death experiencer added, "They say that if you're not a Christian none of you will be able to come in through the eye of the needle, and all that sort of thing. And I think, well, I went up there and I saw it and I certainly wasn't a Christian at the time. So how do they know? So I can't accept it. I've got my own belief and I try to live my way."

It might be easy to conclude that after a near-death experience, the tendency is to adopt a negative attitude toward formal religious practice. But I have not found this to be the case. In fact, nearly 40 percent of the men and women I interviewed were quite active in organized religions prior to their experiences and equally active after them. Some even told me that their NDEs served only to confirm the highest insights of their religious denominations, and this held true for Christian, Jewish, and Buddhist experiencers.

What I believe we can say with surety about near-death experiencers is that they tend to move from an outward approach to religion to an internal one, stressing the importance of an inward closeness to the Divine. I think this explains why so many of them said they preferred to call themselves spiritual people as opposed to religious ones, for what most interested them was the experience of God, rather than the formal observances associated with worshiping God in a communal setting. This shift of focus appears to produce several other related changes in experiencers, among them:

1. A conviction that solitude, prayer, and meditation are more important than organized ritual.
2. A belief that theological dogmas are less important than outward actions. As near-death experiencer Barbara Baird explains:

> I belong to a Christian church, Disciples of Christ, but I'm not into religion or organized theology. I go where the spirit leads me. I'm more interested in what people do than what they think or believe. I examine all religions and kinds of thought to see what works for me in my life.
>
> Before my NDE I was concerned with following the law, God's law, as it was understood in my church, but now I realize I don't have to worry about laws and rules and lists because God wrote all those things on my heart before I was even born. My NDE taught me this, that God has written everything true on our hearts and minds. All we have to do is filter out all the junk and the lies and the garbage. That's why I have a saying: Garbage in, garbage out. I figure that if I can just get rid of the garbage I'll be left with pure spirit. There is a very wonderful phrase in our Bible: "Whatever is true, whatever is pure, whatever is beautiful, think on these things."

3. A yearning to understand others rather than to stand apart from them, which accounts for near-death experiencers' tolerant attitude toward the beliefs and practices of others. It also explains why they are open to many religions. As one experiencer said:

> I belong to a lot of churches. I play the guitar in a Roman Catholic folk group, I'm in the musical group of the

Church of Christ, and I play with the Salvation Army. I'm probably Anglican but it doesn't worry me where I am—it's all God inside me.[2]

In addition to their openness to the beliefs of others, many experiencers become ardent spiritual seekers. Perhaps because they have tasted some of the fruits of a higher spiritual awareness, they desire to know more. I think this explains why so many of those I spoke with told me they gravitated toward the writings of the great mystics, Eastern and Western. Here they found kindred spirits, men and women who had undergone similarly transformative moments in which they felt a closeness with God. Jeffrey Cantor, a Jewish near-death experiencer from Los Angeles, found his spiritual seeking to be something of a paradox:

It's difficult to understand really. Because I know that I encountered the truth in my NDE. Why should I have to go looking any further? I guess what most of us are doing is just looking for ways to experience that same sense of peace and fulfillment here on earth. I mean I've looked to Eastern religions, Christian mystics. Maybe it's insecurity on my part, maybe I'm just looking for stuff to confirm what happened to me. That could be. All I know is that after my NDE, I've been open to exploring anything on the subject of spirituality.

A HIGHER LEVEL OF COMPASSION

As I noted earlier, most near-death experiencers return convinced that at some point in the future they will again be asked to judge themselves in a life-review process. As a result, they not only take their lives more seriously, but remember what else to take seriously. Specifically, that is the love, compassion, and forgiveness they themselves experienced in their NDEs. It is this remembrance of the compassion they encountered in their NDEs that appears to generate within them a heartfelt commitment to lessen the struggles and sufferings of others. Here again is Barbara Baird:

> I don't know how very stingy people who have not helped others are going to face these people they turned their back on. I mean, every one of us is going to have a life review. Everyone has it. And when you do, you feel connected to everything that exists. Maybe this is why when I see things on the TV with children starving, or people at war with each other, like the Serbs and Croats, it makes me very, very sad.

As Baird's story illustrates, another primary change brought about by NDEs is that instead of looking at the world from the standpoint of the isolated self, experiencers view life from the perspective of mutual interdependence. As noted in the previous chapter, this "oversoul awareness" teaches them that if someone else is hurting, they too are hurting, for "We are," as one experiencer put it, "aspects of the perfect whole, and as such are part of God, and of each other." This expanded faculty of compassion helps to explain why so many near-death experiencers emphasize unconditional love, sympathy, and understanding for all creatures as one of the important lessons they learned. Here are some examples:

> One big thing I learned when I died was that we are all part of one big, living universe. If we think we can hurt another person or another living thing without hurting ourselves, we are sadly mistaken.[3]

135

It's the little things—maybe a hurt child that you helped, or just to stop to say hello to a shut-in. Those are the things that are most important.[4]

I was shown what unconditional love is; I was given unconditional love, and once that happens . . . you just can't deliberately hurt another human being.[5]

A POWERFUL SENSE OF PURPOSE

As a result of his experiences and observations as a prisoner in Auschwitz during WW II, the great Austrian psychiatrist Viktor Frankl came to conclude that one of the indispensable keys to finding meaning in life is to live with a sense of purpose. Unfortunately, as Frankl well knew, few of us ever do find a sense of purpose in our lives. Therapists will tell you that the chief cause of depression in America is that many of us simply do not believe our lives have any meaning. One of the most remarkable things I have noted in my conversations with near-death experiencers is how few of them suffer this malaise. After returning from their NDEs, most say they feel as though they have been reborn into a world where their lives have a significant purpose. "I know I am here for a purpose, which is part of God's plan," said one experiencer. "I feel I am here to learn God's law and to love unconditionally. Since my experience, I am no longer content to live for myself. My sense of fulfillment comes from developing my potential for the benefit of service to others, and in this way I also feel I serve God."
Another experiencer said:

All I know is that it's made all the difference to my life. It's given me a purpose and a joy. A determination to help other people. I know I was sent back because I've got work to do for God. I now know that there are laws governing the universe. God does not break these laws, they are part of his own nature. But when we transgress these laws, suffering and disease follow, and the only way to reverse this is to learn to live in harmony with God's laws.[6]

STEWARDSHIP OF THE EARTH

Because they discover—or rediscover—God in their lives, most experiencers arrive at the conclusion that they were put here on earth to respect and care for God's creation. Near-death experiencer Betty Richards told me this:

It makes me sad when human beings are unkind to other creatures who share the earth with us. I always felt a love for animals and nature, but after my NDE I feel even more connected to them, to the cats, to trees, to bushes. That life force, you know. And this connection breeds a higher degree of responsibility for life on earth. It shows me how I must live my life. The Native Americans felt this same level of connection with the life force, and I think we've lost that feeling today. But the NDE seems to bring this respect for the earth back to us in a very elemental way.

This attitude is quite reminiscent of the book of Genesis, where we are told that Adam's primary responsibility when he entered the Garden of Eden was to tend it. A significant number of near-death experiencers I met take this tending of the garden quite seriously; so seriously, in fact, that it infuses their lives with a tremendous sense of mission. Many Christian theologians today call this mission "stewardship of the earth," which is the task of caring for God's creation rather than merely exploiting it for self-aggrandizement or personal profit.

Since no one NDE is identical to another, and because they vary greatly in intensity and depth, it would be wrong to conclude that all who have had near-death experiences are transformed in each of the many ways I have outlined. It is equally true, as I have already noted, that not all near-death experiencers are gifted with the spiritual certitude exhibited by the men and women I have quoted here. Many, in fact, continue to struggle for life direction, with vocational issues, psychological problems, health problems, and so on. They are only human after all. I do not wish to promote the impression that near-death experiencers are living saints or enlightened boddhisattvas, because they are not. Still, my conversations with them have taught me that something miraculous occurs as a result of these encounters with the light. Some who have had near-death experiences eventually forget the lessons they were shown, or deny the validity of their experiences. But for many, like Barbara Baird, the miracle lives on:

> Every once in a while that perfect bright shining world of the NDE pops through to this one. You know, you just see it shining there in the distance, if only for a second, or a moment, and yet it's as wonderful as when you first saw it. That's when you know that this life can be more wonderful too. It's what motivates you to live more spiritually, because the more you do this, the more of heaven on earth you find.

PART THREE

MIRRORS OF THE HEART: MYSTICISM AND THE NEAR-DEATH EXPERIENCE

9

ONE IN ALL, ALL IN ONE: TRUE STORIES OF MYSTICAL EXPERIENCES

∞

Jesus said, if your teachers say to you, "Look, the Kingdom is in heaven," then the birds will get there before you. But the Kingdom is inside you, and is outside you. If you know yourselves, then you will be known; and you will know that you are the sons of the living Father.

—Gospel of Thomas

One in all,
All in one—
If only this is realized,
No more worry about not being perfect!
—Third Patriarch of Zen

At a cocktail party I recently attended, a middle-aged corporate executive asked me to tell him about the book I was writing, as so often happens to me in such situations.

"I'm exploring near-death experiences and their spiritual significance," I told him.

He gave me a peculiar smile, and then said, "Do you really think these people actually die and come back to life?"

"I am the first to admit that near-death experiences do not conclusively prove the existence of life after death," I replied. "But I don't think anyone can deny that the majority of the over eight million people who have had these experiences are fundamentally changed by them. You see, these are people who almost invariably adopt a grateful, spiritual attitude toward life, not simply because they are convinced they encountered God, but because they are certain they were accepted by him. These are no longer issues of belief for these people. They are matters of fact."

The man just smiled, leaned over, and then whispered to me that twenty years earlier he had undergone an out-of-body experience in a hospital that has puzzled him ever since. He also admitted to me that he was afraid to discuss this with too many people, lest they think he had gone mad.

What I didn't tell my friend at the party is that his initial reaction to my book didn't surprise me at all, because it appears that many people focus on NDEs primarily to gain clues about the afterlife, with the result that they pay far less attention to what these experiences can tell us about this life. What they don't see, I believe, is that NDEs are clearly profound moments of spiritual conversion that have much to teach about the potential within us all to live life in fullness. Why this is not more widely recognized is difficult for me to understand, particularly in light of the fact that mystical experiences, which are so very similar to NDEs in every important respect, have long been viewed by scholars of religion as powerful moments of spiritual illumination. Why should we not view NDEs in the same way we view mystical experiences? But before we can address this question, we must look more closely at mystical experiences. What are they? Who has them? How are they similar and dissimilar to NDEs? What do they teach us about God? And how do they change us?

As I shared in the introduction of this book, I was graced

with a mystical experience in 1978. This powerful yet fleeting moment of belonging, oneness, and joy compelled me to look more deeply into the subject of spiritual experiences and led me to the field of comparative religion. One of the things I soon learned after commencing my studies is that mystic moments happen to thousands of people outside the confines of monasteries, convents, and ashrams. In fact, fully one-third of all Americans report that they have had a mystical experience. This statistic has been verified on several occasions by a variety of reputable pollsters, among them the University of Chicago's Dr. Andrew Greeley. In conjunction with the National Opinion Research Center, Greeley found that 18 percent of Americans report having had a mystical experience once or twice in their lives; another 12 percent report they have had several such experiences; and 5 percent say they have had mystical experiences often—for a total of 35 percent.

Another thing I learned about mystical experiences is that they sometimes occur to the most unlikely of people. One of the more illuminating moments of my life, for example, was the day I learned that Dr. Jane Goodall, the eminent British ethologist who has taught us so much about chimpanzee behavior, had been graced with a mystical experience. In 1985 I had asked her to compose an essay on the subject of what she believed for a book I was editing, and when her contribution finally arrived I was more than pleasantly surprised. Here is how she began her essay:

> Some years ago I visited Notre-Dame. By good fortune there were very few people about, and it was still and quiet inside. Just as I was gazing up where the sun made the great rose window glow, the whole cathedral, without warning, was filled with a huge volume of sound. As the organ thundered out Bach's Toccata and Fugue in D minor, the music was alive. The moment, a suddenly cap-

tured moment of eternity, was perhaps the closest I have ever come to experiencing ecstasy, in the sense of the mystic. How could I believe that it was the chance gyrations of bits of primeval dust that had led up to that moment in time—the cathedral soaring to the sky, the collective inspiration and faith of those who caused it to be built, the advent of Bach himself, his brain that had translated truth into music, the mind that could, as mine did then, comprehend the whole inexorable progression of evolution in a split second? Since I could not, and cannot, believe that this was the result of chance, I have to admit antichance. And so I believe in a guiding power in the universe—in other words, I believe in God.[1]

I know that many people come to God in much the same way as Jane Goodall, because during the past decade or so I have interviewed nearly a hundred mystical experiencers. These are men and women who were fortunate enough to connect with life so powerfully that they merged with the Divine, in much the same manner as those who have had near-death experiences. The sixteenth-century mystic, Saint John of the Cross, said that those who have such moments come to enjoy "a certain contact of the soul with divinity; and it is God himself who is then felt and tasted." For those who are convinced they have seen such godly perfection, the end result is always a desire to become better people, to bring into the world some of the light they experienced in their mystic moments. This is why I believe the mystic's encounter with divine love, like that of those who have had near-death experiences, almost invariably spawns spiritual conversion.

How do these mystical encounters with God change people's views about the meaning of life and death? And how do they alter their behavior? Let us turn once again to the experiencers themselves, men and women who told me what it was like for them to encounter God in their mystic moments, and how these encounters changed their lives forever. While you are reading their stories, I encourage you to pay attention not only to the many themes they share in common, but also to those commonalities that connect them to the NDE stories you have read so far. Do these mystical experiences provide men and women with the same kinds of insights into the nature of God, or Ultimate Reality, as NDEs? Do they alter the way they see the world? Do they alter their theology? Do they alter their hopes, their dreams, their very approach to life itself? Do they produce positive results in their lives? These are the many questions I will explore in the following two chapters. But for now, let us listen carefully to the revelations of the mystic.

PAUL PALNIK

He's an artist and nationally known cartoonist who says that his art "swirls around my mystical experiences, of seeing God's eternal light at the core of my soul. That's why I have just two basic themes running through my work: the profundity of being close to God and the absurdity and humor of our lives when we are far from God." He is forty-eight years old and makes his home in Bexley, Ohio, a suburb of Columbus.

I was raised in a Reform Jewish home, and in the fifties and sixties this meant little emphasis on spirituality. In our house, it meant that I knew more about the Cleveland Indians than the Jewish faith. I wanted to be a Jewish American, not a spiritual Jew. Looking back, however, it is clear that I had several mystical moments as a boy, most of which occurred while I was listening to music. Unfortunately, when

I tried to talk about these experiences, my teachers said I was dreaming. And this deeply hurt and humiliated me. So I stopped mentioning my mystical insights to anyone after the age of ten or so. In fact, I stopped having experiences because I wouldn't allow them to happen. I was predisposed to stopping them because I wanted to avoid further ridicule. I came to believe what my parents and teachers taught me: my inner experiences were invalid.

When I finished graduate school I got my first job, teaching art at the University of Arkansas. I was only twenty-two at the time, the youngest faculty member, and I had a lot going for me. But for a variety of personal reasons I was unhappy. I really began to question who I was, if I was being true to myself, and I found that I wasn't. That's when I had the most profound experience of my life, which nothing yet has equalled. I was doing some reading, half-watching TV at the same time, and I grew tired and began to relax. I had a big cushy pillow, and I lay down and began reading the part in the Bible where Abraham looked up to the stars, fell down on his face, and God revealed himself and said, "I will make your seed as countless as the stars in the heavens." This was surprising, because I never, ever read the Bible. But my unhappiness caused me to reexamine my Judaism.

I spent a few moments trying to figure out what the narrative meant. What did God mean, "I will make your seed as countless as the stars in the heavens?" I put the book aside, closed my eyes, and lay down. I then fell into the deepest mystical moment I have ever had. Suddenly it was clear to me that I had been denying my soul and my spiritual self; that I had, for the past several years, been untrue to God. Then this door to the inner mind just flung open, crashed open, and I had this profound vision of a pure light, not in the sense of a metaphor, but a tangible white light. This light was so holy and profound that I was awestruck. There was a clear communication that it was alive and relating to me without words. What I felt was this enormous peace and instantaneous heavenly knowing, and I wanted to die. I remember thinking, if this is heaven, I want to go. I want to be absorbed into this light—brighter than bright, lighter than light, more alive than life. It is impossible to describe, almost like a liquid light, like a billowing, living light in the blackest black floating in space. I just wanted to merge into it, to become one with this holy, living eternal light.

I know I saw God. He revealed himself to me. That was more than twenty years ago, and you are only the fourth person I have shared this with. I mean, this isn't the sort of thing you tell people. How do you tell someone that you saw and communicated with God? I do feel strongly that this experience imparted a higher knowledge to me. Not the belief in God, but rather the certainty of God's existence. You know, it's like looking at a photo of New York. You may have an idea of what you think the city is about, but if you have never been there it's not until you actually walk the streets of Manhattan that you really know New York. So now I understand what is meant in the Torah when it says that Moses came face-to-face with God. I know what that narrative means now. After this experience, it became clear to me, without a question of doubt, that within the innermost part of me, the innermost part of everyone, re-sides God. God-light is in everyone. Beyond any individual, beyond any religion, beyond any planets, beyond anything, anywhere, there is always and forever God—the eternal intelligent light that is running everything. After that experience, I knew the universe was one, the mind was one, we are all one entity. God is absolutely one. I know from experience.

This mystical moment changed me for the rest of my life. I remember that the first thing I did was run over to the University of Arkansas library. I searched every book I could about religious experiences. To my great relief, I found similar stories in all religions. I first discovered a clear exposition of what happened to me in the Upanishads, then in the Zohar, then in the writings of the Christian mystics, then in Buddhism. It made me feel like I instantly went from being a madman to a blessed man, because I knew that what had happened to me was universally regarded as sacred, rather than a doorway to the madhouse. I sat alone in a corner of the library and cried with an overflowing heart.

Today, some twenty-five years later, I'm very comfortable with this. I became a religious man, not in the sense of showing up at a building every week, or in the born-again sense of feeling I've been saved and converted to the truth, but in the sense that I know God exists and that I am and will be a part of Him forever. I still go to the synagogue every week, I'm a practicing Jew, but I'm just as close to any spiritual person as I am to a Jew. Denominations don't mean a great deal to me. If you get up high enough, you can see everybody together, and that is what happens to you in a mystical experience. It's like the astronauts floating in space above the earth, looking down. You feel that your soul is a part of every soul. And when you know that to be true, the only thing to do is live with a lot of love, creativity, honesty, and kindness. In my view, the only way to do this well is to practice the art of living in the present. People say, "Hey, one day at a time," but I take that even further. I say, "Live one *now* at a time." Anything short of that is not reality, because this exact moment is your destiny. Your soul is rooted in the eternal light. Become who you must become. Come home. The eternal presence of God will guide you.

CLAUDIA MICHELE

She is trained as a vocational guidance counselor, workshop leader, and psychotherapist. Much of her time is devoted to contemplation. She works and makes her home in the suburbs of Pittsburgh.

I was twenty-four when I had my first mystical experience, which I call the "revelations." This was back in 1980, when I was a student. It was a difficult time in my life because I was nearing the end of my graduate study in counselor education, suffering from a bout with anorexia, and temporarily separated from my husband. I was emotionally and physically filled with turmoil, questions, and a deep desire to finally figure out what life is all about. I remember that I told myself I'd be willing to die for an answer.

It all came to a boiling point in May of 1980, and this is when I had my revelations. I was washing dishes, of all things, when suddenly my personality literally dissolved in an instantaneous merging with an infinite compassionate universal intelligence. I have no idea how this happened, but an exquisite bliss just came over me, and it filled me with calmness and peace. In that instant I changed. Gone were the questions of why was I here, what is life about, all those things, because everything became obvious in the dissolution of separateness from all things. This universal relatedness at the core of everything wiped away all my fears, because I saw that my fate was all part of the scheme of things, and that everything was perfect as it was, as it was meant to be.

It has always been difficult to actually describe what I experienced, because words can't do justice to it. The image that first came to me when I was trying to explain my new knowledge to a friend was that of that tacky light fixture they use in discos and ballrooms: that giant, rotating ball of tiny reflective mirrors, each a unique piece of glass reflecting different experiences caught in its unique angle of reflection, all eventually moving in the same direction, all energized by the same force, but whose experience remains completely unique to their angle, their time. But of course this doesn't come close to what I actually witnessed. Words just can't describe the ultimate.

This may sound grandiose, but I believe this revelation of the Divine temporarily made me a receptacle of infinite knowledge. For there in front of me, within me, and around me was what I can only describe with imagery: a brilliant, sparkling, infinite, unified universe. This revelation of the Divine in all things caused me to be struck with dumb-founded awe. It was as though my mind had suddenly engulfed the entirety of all experience, not just my own, but the past, present, and future of "all things," every possibility and impossibility.

I knew in that glorious instant that I had the opportunity to die in the body and join my consciousness with the supra-consciousness; join spirit with spirit in infinite, eternal union. I could merge blissfully with "all things" or play out the term of my life. The choice was mine. I knew just as instantly that it didn't matter what choice I made, because death was nothing more than the fearless passing from one state to another.

In addition to this came the insight that there is no human authority. None. No president or priest, counselor or doctor can provide us with what we are not ready to experience. That, I now see, is the whole point of the saying, "If you meet the Buddha on the road, kill him." Because if anyone assumes they have the answers for you, they are a false messiah. In a universe of unity, nobody is more or less than anybody else. This is when I came to see that self-trust and relentless personal responsibility in life are absolutely essential to those who would have the courage to live spiritually.

At some point toward the end of my experience, I felt impelled by a commandment to "Put it in the living." I can't say where it came from, because I don't recall being spoken to by anyone, but this just came to me: "Put it in the living." I took this to mean that the validity for life was found entirely in the moment; that whatever or wherever one happened to be, that conscious participation in the present alone was what mattered. I came to realize that this was the definition of truth itself, and that it was also the definition of beauty. I took this to mean that what I needed to do in life was simply to live each moment with honesty and passion from my perspective, or as I've since read in a book, "Love God, and do what you like!" This means that if you genuinely love God, you do not intentionally harm any of the manifestations he has chosen to put into your life, including yourself.

It has been some fifteen years since the revelations, and I am still capable of experiencing its fruits, or at least capable of accessing the feelings it gave me, simply by repeating the phrase "all things." "All things" has come to mean God to me. When I think about "All things" I am suddenly able to see life from many perspectives. This enables me to affirm those things that I find most enhancing in life, so I gravitate toward them effortlessly. That's really the goal of my spiritual life, to gravitate toward those things that enhance the quality of my existence rather than detract from it.

In the process of learning to be honest with myself about what nurtured my growth and what did not, I let go of the anorexia, and my husband and I were divorced. I devoted my life to encouraging others to discover in what unique ways they are expressions of "all things"—or the universe—and how they can contribute those creative aspects of themselves to their environments. In other words, how they, too, can "put it in the living."

The ability to experience empathy has taken on a whole new meaning since the revelations and has enhanced my ability as a counselor tremendously. My relationships with my mother and sister have reached a level of mutual understanding totally unforeseen. It just seems that empathy or compassion, along with a sense of humor, seems to naturally flow in my life. Since the revelations, everywhere I look I see myself. There I go: that bald man, this angry child, that fearful cat, that cool stone, that bubbling brook, that worm struggling for its life, that bird desperate to feed her hungry babies, that one trapped in his rage, this one anxious but fearful of finding out why. Hardly strangers! Empathy is the life of the soul, I think, because the soul that allows us to see the one in the other is the soul that finds joy. The more starved the soul, the greater the inability to see that connectedness, to accommodate the one in the other.

I've often thought, Wouldn't it be wonderful if people woke up each day and instead of thinking, "Christ, another damn day," their reaction was, "Christ! Another damn wonderful day!" Wouldn't that be great. That's how I've been trying to live since my revelations. It isn't easy, of course, and I continue to get frustrated when I fail to respond joyfully to life. But I am convinced that every single thing, every last possible combination of things, every space between spaces, every moment, every thought and series of thoughts, every pain and every wailing, every breath and sound itself, is a manifestation of God. Each thing is a unique emanation of God.

When I feel most connected to this universal life, I am imbued with ecstasy. In telling this to you, I am transported in image and memory into the heart of my understanding of what it is to be human, to be conscious, to be humbled in reverence and gratitude. This moment that we eternalize by experiencing it, that we incorporate into the record of creation, is so precious and fleeting. So I say, dance that dance! Sing that unmatched song! Make a joyful noise!

DR. ALFRED PAINTER

Dr. Painter is a retired Methodist minister and philosophy professor who makes his home in the mountains of southern Utah. He lives there with his wife, Anita, who is a champion senior swimmer, and a large family of dogs and horses. He is eighty-one years old.

When I was eighteen years old I lived on Queen Anne Hill in Seattle, which is a good-sized hill near the center of the city. My favorite pastime was to climb to the park at the top of the hill to sit and watch the city below and the surrounding mountains to the west. One day at dusk, a particularly clear and unusually sunny day, I became entranced by the movement around me and my mind began to tune into the complex, integrated mass of movement of the humans below me, all interconnected in various ways. I found myself caught up in it as a part of my own being.

I remember, for example, that I became aware of the lights turning off and on in the official buildings downtown as well as in the residential areas. I became aware of the red taillights on cars leaving the city as well as of the headlights of cars coming toward the city. Rapidly, I became aware of the many other forms of interconnectedness. In the distance there were planes coming and going from the international airport. In my mind's eye I saw people from all over the world arriving in Seattle, and leaving it, and I personally felt this massive interconnectedness of life. I saw passenger trains coming and going. I became aware of the towers in the distance sending out radio waves connecting us to others around the globe. It occurred to me that the vast, sprawling city was really like a living organism with the coming and going of the people flowing like blood through the vessels of the planet—and I was an integral part of it.

Somehow, the overpowering awareness of my inevitable involvement with this mass of interconnected life temporarily dissolved my sense of separateness and aloneness, and I was swept away with an immense feeling of joy and belonging. I was so swept up, in fact, that when I finally "came to my senses" and perceived myself as an isolated human being again, I laughed at the thought. The walls that separated me from the world dissolved and a great weight was lifted from my shoulders. Sensing the surge of life in everything around me, I knew, for the first time in my life, that I really did belong to the world and that everything was as it should be.

I credit this mystical moment for redirecting my life away from a career in business toward a career in teaching and the ministry, because it wasn't long after this that I entered the University of Chicago to obtain my Ph.D. in philosophy. I later became a Methodist minister. I also credit this experience for something a great deal more profound than simply directing my career, because since the day I had that mystical experience I have never felt alone or left out at any time. And I have never doubted that when things get bleak, the problems I face are those of my own creation, which result from an inability to see or act upon all of the possible supporting changes that surround and connect me to what I like to call the "is-ness of life." I lost my first wife of thirty years to Alzheimer's disease when I was in my sixties. And then I lost my cherished daughter in my seventies. Through it all, I have come to accept the universe for what it is, and this has brought me peace.

Now I am in my eighties, living here in the mountains of

Utah, where I retired with my second wife, Anita, just two years ago. I spend my days walking in the woods with our dogs, meditating on the clouds and sky and mountains, and luxuriating in the beauty of what I call this great outdoor church. I know that the years ahead of me are few, but I do not fear death, because I know from my mystical experience that, whatever may come, it can only serve as an opening to still greater involvement with the eternal is-ness of life, which I am more than happy to call God.

When you get to be my age, people often ask you what you've learned, and the truth is, I learned most of what I needed to know back on Queen Anne Hill over sixty years ago. As anyone who has had a mystical experience will tell, life is an endless adventure moved along by many forces that are beyond our control, but one which we can give ourselves over to in trust and confidence. There is always more going on than we are equipped to perceive through our limited senses and with our limited experience. This "more," I believe, is the root of religious or spiritual life. Change is at the bottom of it, and the more we are a part of it—the more we rely and trust in it—the more likely are we to uncover the pleasures and mysteries of living.

Here in the last lap of life, I am utterly convinced that life's meaning isn't found in what we have achieved or accumulated. It is found in our ability to express our uniqueness in this unified world of divine light and intelligence to which we will always belong. Wherever I am, you see, I am home. So I face each day with a deep sense of awe, content to let be what will be: the universe is ever unfolding before my eyes, and I see that it is good.

10

TRANSLUCENT WINDOWS: MYSTICAL EXPERIENCES AND NDES IN COMPARATIVE PERSPECTIVE

∞

Man's walled mind has no access to a ladder upon which he can, on his own strength, rise to knowledge of God. Yet his soul is endowed with translucent windows that open to the beyond. And if he rises to reach out to Him, it is a reflection of the Divine light in him that gives him the power for such yearning.

—Rabbi Abraham Joshua Heschel

In the course of my research for this (and other) books, I have learned that a good many Americans associate mysticism with the offbeat and the bizarre. A handful of the people I interviewed were even convinced that mysticism is a dangerous esoteric practice pursued exclusively "by New Age cultists," as a man in Oxford, Mississippi, told me. But there is nothing "New Age" about mysticism. Nearly identical stories to the ones we have just read have been recorded for many centuries. While the language and symbols mystics have used to describe and interpret their encounters with

God have changed much over the years, the core experience has remained virtually unchanged; what mystics reported three thousand years ago they also report today.

No, mysticism is not "New Age" spirituality. It is old-age faith. As a wise scholar once insightfully declared, "Mysticism is to religion what basic research is to science." When you compare sacred scriptures the world over, it is difficult to disagree with this statement. Jesus, Buddha, Mohammed, Shankara—each of these religious prophets was also obviously a mystic, or so it seems to me. When Jesus said that "The Kingdom of God is within you," for example, he sounds very much like a person who has encountered God directly in a mystic moment. When the Buddha exclaimed to his followers that "within this fathom-high body . . . lies the world and the rising of the world and the ceasing of the world," he, too, exposed the soul of a mystic. When Mohammed announced that "Wherever you turn is God's face," he revealed a mystical nature as well. And when the great eighth-century Indian sage Shankara said that "Liberation cannot be achieved except by the perception of the identity of the individual spirit with the universal spirit," he revealed to his disciples that he too knew much about the mystery, wonder, and dynamism that animates and perpetually connects us to this universe in which we live.

I think it is fair to say that mysticism is the well from which good theology springs. It is nothing to be feared, then, but rather something to be revered. Unfortunately, mysticism is all too often viewed by people today as an escapist religious practice that eventually leads to little more than a self-centered form of spiritual dementia. The truth, however, is that mysticism is really nothing more than the practice of achieving a deeper harmony or connectedness with life itself. Those whom we call mystics are simply people who have been able to do this with tremendous success. The most fortunate among them are able to connect with life so powerfully that they occasionally report a merger with the Divine, in much the same manner as those who have had near-death experiences.

When you stop to think about it, we are all actually engaged in the same activity as the mystic—this perpetual attempt to connect ourselves meaningfully to the wider world—for the bulk of our waking hours. As I write these lines, for example, my little son is downstairs in the basement playing with a friend from the neighborhood. Together, these two five-year-old boys are attempting to connect with one another through play, and it is through this play that they celebrate the joy of living. As so many mystics have observed, God is most often met in the joy we feel from connecting powerfully with life itself. I believe this is why the root of the word *religion* means "to bind," or "to connect," because connections bring us joy and meaning, while disconnections do much the opposite.

I believe we are all, to a greater or lesser degree, mystics; we are born mystics, in fact, because each of us has the capacity to experience moments when we feel deeply connected to life. Regardless of whether or not we have had a life-changing mystical experience or NDE, and regardless of whether or not we "believe in God," we all enjoy—or certainly desire to enjoy—moments when we feel a tremendous sense of belonging and affinity to life. We know that it is in these moments that we feel good about ourselves and are happy to be alive. It is these experiences which make life meaningful. This is why I believe the only truly significant difference between these people we call mystics and the rest of us is simply that they take their mystic moments quite seriously, while the rest of us forget them, or perhaps just write them off as inexplicable episodes of joy. In other words, unlike most of us, mystics live with the conviction that these revelatory experiences of oneness and belonging provide them with significant hints about the potential that lies within us all to experience the glory of life.

THE ANATOMY OF MYSTICAL EXPERIENCES

A tremendous amount of scholarly writing has been generated on the subject of mysticism, the bulk of which appeared prior to the 1970s. The most influential scholar on the subject was Harvard University's eminent psychologist William James, who, between 1890 and 1915, wrote prolifically about mysticism. After studying hundreds of stories from men and women who had undergone mystical experiences, James was struck by the fact that nearly all of them were describing precisely the same things. James observed that such a similarity of experience "ought to make a critic stop and think." Just as many of us are struck today by the enormous similarity of ND accounts, James was fascinated by the resemblance of mystical experiences, and this compelled him to study the subject intensively. In his famous Gifford Lectures, delivered at the University of Edinburgh in 1901, James first proposed "four marks which, when an experience has them, may justify us calling it mystical. . . ." They are:

1. *Ineffability.* The mystic declares that his experience "defies expression, that no adequate report of its contents can be given in words."
2. *Noetic quality.* (The word *noetic* is derived from the Greek word *nous*, which is best translated as "mind" or "knowing.") James felt that mystical experiences were "states of insight into depths of truth unplumbed by the discursive intellect."
3. *Transiency.* Mystical states cannot be sustained for long.

4. *Passivity.* During the mystic moment the "mystic feels as if his own will were in abeyance, and indeed sometimes as if he were grasped and held by a superior power."

It is difficult not to notice that James's four marks of the mystical experience also characterize the most profound NDEs.

Expanding upon James's work, such scholars of mysticism as Evelyn Underhill, Aldous Huxley, and W. T. Stace delved more deeply into the experiential content of mysticism. And although they arrived at somewhat different findings, they all agreed that mysticism is an easily recognizable pattern of human thought and experience, most often characterized by five principle features. These five features are so obviously prevalent in the majority of NDEs, and the accounts of the mystics who report them are so similar to the stories we have heard from those who have had near-death experiences, that I outline them here.

1. Unity with God

As the stories we read in the previous chapter show, a sense of oneness with God and creation is referred to repeatedly by mystics. As the third-century Roman philosopher and mystic Plotinus wrote: "In this seeing, we neither hold an object nor trace distinction; there is no two. The man is changed, no longer himself nor self-belonging; he is merged with the Supreme, sunken into it, one with it. . . ." A similar experience of unity compelled the ancient Buddhist mystic Sen T'sen to write: "When the Ten Thousand things are viewed in their oneness, we return to the Origin and remain where we have always been." An eloquent contemporary account of this experience of oneness was recently shared with me by Boyce Batey, a courtly sixty-year-old man who had a powerful mystical experience shortly after his graduation from Princeton in the summer of 1954:

I had just finished reading William Wordsworth's *The Prelude*, and I decided to consciously try and focus my mind so that I could achieve the same ineffable sense of awe and beauty and oneness with the universe that the author had described. I tried many times to focus my mind on various objects, and to finely attune my senses to the things around me, but to no avail. After several failed attempts at this, however, suddenly and without trying, my consciousness was in another plane or dimension of reality. A great white light surrounded me completely and was within me and outside of me at the same time. I was that light, that light was me. That light was God and I was God. I was one with all and all was one with me. Everything outside of me was God and I was God; everything within was God and I was God.

Another mystical experiencer, Robert Cubin, who makes his home in Harrogate, England, told me:

It is impossible to describe this exquisite feeling of unity except to say that "I" seemed no longer to exist and that "I" was now an integral part of everything else. All my worries had gone and I realized that the blissful feeling of total peace came directly from the "oneness." This all took place in the presence of an invading bluish-white light, which appeared to come from everywhere, as though every molecule in the room was radiating light. I felt as though I came into contact with the simple, naked truth. I sank into the exquisite oneness.

161

The perception of unity described by Boyce Batey and Robert Cubin is often expressed in Hinduism through the well-known phrase, *"tat tvam asi,"* or "that art Thou," which means essentially that the individual self is one with God, and vice-versa. The sixteenth-century mystic, Saint Catherine of Genoa, surely understood the meaning of tat tvam asi when she exclaimed, "My Me is God, nor do I recognize any other Me except my God Himself." Many mistakenly view such statements as outright expressions of unbridled egotism, spiritual self-delusion, or, at the very least, rude affronts to the Creator. How can each of us be God? But this is not what mystics are saying, because mysticism is actually about *losing* the self, which is the furthest thing from egotism. What mystics do say is that each of us (indeed everything in the entire universe) is part of God. It is this understanding of unity, this belief in the essential oneness of God with all creation, that prompted the twelfth-century French mystic Saint Bernard to write that, "In those respects in which the soul is unlike God, it is also unlike itself."

2. Self-Transcendence

Like the near-death experiencers we met in previous chapters, mystics repeatedly report that they expand so greatly in consciousness that the normal limitations of their senses are greatly surpassed. As Boyce Batey told me, during his mystical experience his consciousness appeared to exist "in another plane or dimension of reality. There was in me . . . a quality in consciousness that I have never before nor since experienced. . . . It was as though I was aware of the laws of the universe and the meaning of existence. I transcended all of the normal limitations of the material self until there were no boundaries at all between me and that which was not me; all was one."

This ability to transcend the self and its limitations appears to enable the mystic to encounter the greater reality of God, just as it does for those who have had near-death experiences. I believe this is why so many mystics and near-death experiencers have stressed, as the fourteenth-century German mystic Meister Eckhart did, that "if the soul is to know God, it must forget itself . . . for as long as it is self-aware and self-conscious, it will not see or be conscious of God. But when, for God's sake, it becomes unselfconscious and lets go of everything, it finds itself again in God."

3. Timelessness

Like the majority of near-death experiencers, mystics often report a disorientation in time and space. Boyce Batey, for example, in his mystical experience, found that "There was no past or future; all time was now." Over and over mystics stress that their experiences bring them in touch with a timeless reality. This must explain why so many of them stress that what is important in life is to perceive the "timeless now" of the divine present. "To men alone, time is elusive; to men with God time is eternity in disguise," wrote the great twentieth-century philosopher Rabbi Abraham Joshua Heschel. This same conviction compelled the thirteenth-century Sufi mystic and poet Jalāl al-Dīn al-Rumī to conclude that "Past and future veil God from our sight." Meister Eckhart agreed. "Time," he wrote, "is what keeps the light from reaching us. There is no greater obstacle to God than time."

4. Ecstasy

As we saw in the stories in the previous chapter, mystics nearly always express feelings of love, joy, and ecstasy as a result of their encounters with God. Here is Shankara, the eighth-century Indian mystic and philosopher, writing of his mystical ecstasy:

The ego has disappeared. I have realized my identity with Brahma, and so all my desires have melted away. I have risen above my ignorance and my knowledge of this seeming universe. What is this joy that I feel? How shall I measure it? I know nothing but joy, limitless, unbounded!

Mystical experiencer Robert Cubin told me this:

A feeling of calmness, peace, and tranquility, such as I had never known, enveloped me entirely. The overriding feeling I had was a combination of unconditional, perfect love, peace, and complete unity with everything. . . . I remained in a state of perfect bliss.

Boyce Batey spoke with equal passion:

There was in my being a sense of love, peace, joy, and exultation in dimensions and quality that I have never before nor since experienced. . . . I knew that the drift of the cosmos ultimately was toward good, that there was no evil in the universe, that there was no death, that all was life and life was God and God was love and that I was God."

5. Conversion

William James found that the deeper and more profound the mystical experience a person has, the more significant an impact it will have on converting their perceptions, values, and behavior. I believe this is also true with regard to NDEs. James also came to see that powerful moments of spiritual illumination generate a new form of faith in those who undergo them. This explains why both NDEs and mystical experiences must be classified as conversionary. Speaking of her own mystical conversion, Saint Catherine of Genoa cried out simply, "No more sins." Twentieth-century Quaker mystic Rufus Jones described his spiritual conversion in language similar to that of many who have had near-death experiences:

> I remember kneeling down alone in a beautiful forest glade and dedicating myself then and there in the quiet and silence, but in the presence of an invading light, to the work of interpreting the deeper nature of the soul and its relation to God. . . . A sense of mission broke in on me and I felt I was being called. . . .

Of course, many other things can and often do occur within mystical experiences other than these five features. But when you compare the statements of mystics through the ages to those of the contemporary mystics I have quoted, these same five features always appear, regardless of an experiencer's sex, race, religion, or national origin. These same five features of the mystical experience also appear in most, if not all, NDEs. I would even go so far as to say that if an NDE does not contain all of these five elements it should not be classified as a complete NDE.

There are really only two significant differences between mystical experiences and NDEs. The first is that NDEs are generally precipitated by a traumatic physical crisis, which is not always the case with mystical experiences. The second difference is that mystical experiences normally occur while people are fully conscious, whereas NDEs generally occur while people are unconscious, or out-of-body.

The many commonalities that unite these two varieties of spiritual experience far outweigh the minor differences that distinguish them from one another. I say this because I agree wholeheartedly with William James that the actual "fruits" of these experiences are a great deal more significant than their "roots," or causes. In other words, asking why spiritual experiences occur is a far less meaningful question than, "How do spiritual experiences change our lives?" While the first question is difficult if not impossible to answer, the second one is not. Mystical experiences and NDEs nearly always produce the same result: people return from these profound moments of illumination with a new understanding of what it means to be human, and an ardent desire to change themselves for the better. The question is: Do they really become better people? Do mystical experiences and NDEs actually promote psychological and spiritual well-being? Or do they have a negative effect on mental health? It is to these questions we turn in the following chapter.

11

HEALING VISIONS: NDES, MYSTICAL EXPERIENCES, AND PSYCHOLOGICAL HEALTH

∞

Among all my patients in the second half of life—that is to say, over thirty-five—there has not been one whose problem in the last resort was not that of finding a religious outlook on life. It is safe to say that every one of them fell ill because he had lost that which living religions of every age have given their followers, and none of them has been really healed who did not regain this religious outlook. This of course has nothing whatever to do with a particular creed or membership of a church.

—Carl G. Jung

Although millions of people have undergone spiritual experiences similar to the ones we have seen in this book, there are those who remain skeptical of their ultimate value. Boyce Batey, for example, said that when he told his atheist mother-in-law about his mystical experience, she exclaimed confidently, "You just overloaded your circuits and blew a fuse." Whether she was right about that may never be answered to everyone's satisfaction, but several social-scientific studies have concluded that "peak experiences"—whether mystical or near-death—unequivocally change people for the better.

In a variety of studies he conducted in the 1970s, for example, Dr. Ralph Hood, Professor of Psychology at the University of Tennessee, found that individuals reporting mystical experiences performed significantly better than average on a variety of tests showing mental health. He concluded that mystical experiences are neither pathologic nor escapist (as some Freudian analysts once argued), but actually lead to healthier and more stable personalities. As he wrote, "It is clear that the person reporting mystical experience may be described as one with a breadth of interest, creative and innovative, tolerant of others, socially adept, and unwilling to accept simple solutions to problems."[1]

Two decades before Dr. Hood published the results of his research, Abraham Maslow was equally convinced that peak experiences promoted greater psychological health. He arrived at this conclusion because he found that such experiences came most often to "the best people, in their best moments, under the best conditions." In *Motivation and Personality*, his study of psychologically healthy, self-actualized men and women—such as Albert Schweitzer, Abraham Lincoln, and Aldous Huxley—Dr. Maslow isolated twelve personal characteristics these extraordinary "peakers" (as he liked to call them) held in common. In 1990, the distinguished British philosopher David Lorimer noted how very similar these twelve "clinically observed characteristics" of psychologically healthy men and women are with those of the average person who has had a near-death experience or mystical experience. For instance, according to Maslow, self-actualized people obtain a "clearer, more efficient perception of reality." This clearly corresponds with near-death experiencers and mystical experiencers' stated ability to see things from many perspectives, to stand back and examine life more objectively and fairly. It also corresponds with the "oversoul" quality that occurs in these experiences, the ability to view things from a wider, or higher, perspective, from which it is possible to see things and their interrelationships more clearly.

Moreover, self-actualizers develop an "increased acceptance of self, others, and of nature," writes Maslow. This corresponds with near-death experiencers' and mystical experiencers' commitment to unconditional love, stewardship of the earth, and general acceptance of themselves and their role as human beings.

In addition, Maslow believed that self-actualized men and women were more "spontaneous, natural, and unconventional." As we have seen in the stories so far, near-death experiencers and mystical experiencers say they become less concerned with what others think of them and are therefore more content to be who they are. Unbounded by fixed patterns of social and religious expectation, they say they are freer to do what comes naturally to them.

Self-actualizers also become "problem-centering" rather than self-centering people. This was certainly true for most of the near-death experiencers and mystical experiencers with whom I spoke. Because they return from their experiences with a strong sense of mission and purpose, they want to become problem solvers rather than problem makers. In addition, many near-death experiencers say that as a result of their life reviews they understand that a great many problems originate in a simple lack of compassion and empathy for the struggles and suffering of others.

Maslow also insisted that the majority of self-actualizers live with an increased sense of "detachment and a desire for privacy." Earlier I noted that many near-death experiencers and mystical experiencers come to cherish atmospheres of solitude and privacy apart from the clamor of our noisy world. Such solitude enables them to reconnect themselves with a deeper reality.

An increased spirit of "autonomy, and resistance to acculturation" also characterize psychologically healthy men and women according to Maslow. Those who have had near-death experiences exhibit these traits as well, not only because they feel confident about who they are and what is important in life, but because they try to remain open to knowledge from any quarter. Many refuse to be pigeonholed into a single group, or to allow themselves to become swept away by a popular movement.

There is a "greater freshness of appreciation, and richness of emotional reactions" among self-actualized people, says Maslow. Here again, many near-death experiencers and mystical experiencers believe that as a result of their unitive moments they see the world through sacred eyes. They return with an enhanced appreciation and respect for life. Most say they wish only to live fully in the present.

Maslow also believed that self-actualized people have a "higher frequency of peak experiences." He was unable to provide a great deal of evidence for this in his time, but since then, Dr. Mihaly Csikszentmihali of the University of Chicago certainly has. In his engaging book *Flow: The Psychology of Optimal Experience* (1992), Dr. Csikszentmihali provides an abundance of evidence indicating that self-actualized people are in a state of "flow" more often than psychologically unhealthy people. The flow state is described by Csikszentmihali as "a sense of exhilaration, a deep sense of enjoyment that is long cherished and that becomes a landmark memory for what life should be like." He goes on to stress that those who regularly experience such flow are people who manage to solve the problem of meaning because their individual purpose "merges with the universal flow." This sounds very much like a mystical moment to me.

Psychologically healthy men and women also develop "an increased identification with the human species," says Maslow. This clearly corresponds with near-death experiencers' and mystical experiencers' growth of compassion, commitment to unconditional love, and forgiveness of others. An increased sense of identification and compassion for others is also the result of near-death experiencers' and mystical experiencers' apprehension of unity.

Maslow also believed that "changed or improved interpersonal relations" also characterize healthy men and women. Many near-death experiencers and mystical experiencers told me that their relationships with others became richer and deeper as a result of their experiences. Yet, as Phyllis Atwater has pointed out in her two books on the aftereffects of NDEs, some experiencers also initially encounter strained relations with their family and friends.

Self-actualized people, according to Maslow, develop a "more democratic character structure," by which he means that they adopt an open and friendly attitude toward others, regardless of their race, religion, or social status. This openness, this tendency not to judge people too quickly, is one of the significant aftereffects of NDEs and mystical experiences.

"Greatly increased creativity" is another common trait among self-actualized people. This corresponds to near-death experiencers' and mystical experiencers' sense of mission and desire to use all of their abilities to improve the world around them.

Finally, Maslow was convinced that self-actualizers are more "open to experience." This correlates with my observation that near-death experiencers and mystical experiencers thirst for wisdom, are open to new ideas and religions, and are willing to listen to the beliefs of others. Because they believe in unconditional love, they are not defensive people, but open people.

These numerous correlations between psychologically healthy men and women and those who undergo NDEs or mystical experiences are tremendously difficult to deny.

Clearly, both of these extraordinary spiritual experiences move people toward greater emotional health. They transform us for the better, not only because they change the way we view ourselves in a healthy direction, but because they alter the way we view others and the world in a positive manner. They also release our creative resources, allow us to become more open and spontaneous, and convince us, beyond a shadow of a doubt, that life is worthwhile, something to be savored and enjoyed, validated and cared for with all the reserves of passion that lie within us.

12

THE JOURNEY HOME,
AN ETERNAL THEOLOGY

The nature of these revelations is the same; they are perceptions of the absolute law.

—Ralph Waldo Emerson

You are the light of the world.

—Jesus (Matthew 5:14)

The universal nucleus of every known high religion . . . has
been the private, lonely, personal illumination, revelation, or
ecstasy of some acutely sensitive prophet or seer.

—Abraham Maslow

In addition to concluding that peak moments make us psychologically healthier, Dr. Abraham Maslow also found that
those who undergo peak experiences nearly always come to
adopt the "eternal spiritual values" profiled in the sacred
texts of the world's religions. This finding eventually led
him to conclude that Albert Einstein was absolutely right
when he wrote that

The most beautiful and profound emotion we can experience is the sensation of the mystical. It is the sower of all

true science. He to whom this emotion is a stranger, who can no longer wonder and stand in rapt awe, is as good as dead. To know that what is impenetrable to us really exists, manifesting itself as the highest wisdom and most radiant beauty, which our dull faculties can comprehend only in their primitive forms—this knowledge, this feeling, is at the center of true religion.

If Einstein and Maslow are right, and I believe they are, the values embedded in the world's religions emerged primarily from peak experiences. And if this is so, then mystical experiences and NDEs are nothing less than the soul of religious theology the world over, for theology, at heart, is little more than the intellectual attempt to express the meaning and significance of what it means to encounter God—and to live as though we have. Who has described the most powerful encounters with God in human history? Mystics and those who have had near-death experiences.

The central question of religion has remained the same since the dawn of recorded history: How do we connect more profoundly with God? Morality, ethics, prayer, meditation, contemplation, ritual, and worship are all responses to this single question. Each of the stories we have read from those who have had near-death experiences and mystical experiencers has focused on this question as well.

Yet, as we all know, a single question can get you a thousand different answers, which is why we have many religions on earth rather than one. I have long viewed this religious diversity as a wondrous thing, for what could be more fascinating than to survey the ongoing, worldwide quest to find meaning through exploration into the mystery we call God? However, like many others, I have also been interested in isolating those themes that the world's religions have in common. Putting aside minor theological differences of ritual and worship, is there a core theology we can point to with confidence? And if so, are there shared lessons to explore? Is there common ground at the source of religious faith the world over?

The esteemed British philosopher Aldous Huxley certainly felt so. In the 1940s he argued persuasively that if we stripped away the artifice of the world's religions to study only the sayings of the great seers and prophets who encountered God directly through personal revelations (mystical, near-death, or otherwise), we would find a "perennial philosophy." More recently, the distinguished University of California comparative religionist Huston Smith undertook a similar investigation, which resulted in a stunning yet seldom read book entitled *Forgotten Truth*, a scholarly study of the ancient theologies that reside at the heart of the world's religions. Like Huxley, Professor Smith concluded that underlying the superficial differences that distinguish the world's many religions we find a remarkable "underlying unity."

What we also find, I'm convinced, is a remarkable underlying unity between this "perennial philosophy" (which I much prefer to call the eternal theology) and the statements of the near-death experiencers and mystical experiencers we have met so far.

While more pages have been written about the quest for God than any other subject in human history, the eternal theology that unites the world's religions is surprisingly uncomplicated. It begins with the assumption, well stated by so many near-death experiencers and mystical experiencers, that everything in the universe is the product of God's grace, which means that all of creation is essentially beautiful, orderly, and unified, as opposed to ugly and chaotic—good rather than bad. As it is written in the Bible, "And God looked at everything that he made, and behold, it was very good." Or, as near-death experiencer Dr. George Rodonaia said earlier, "I felt a wholeness with the light; a sense that

175

everything is right with me and the universe. . . . God showed me that the universe in which we live is a beautiful and marvelous mystery that is connected together forever and for always."

In the Upanishads it is written that "Whatever lives is full of the Lord." The Bible, likewise, tells us that everything is fueled by the "breath of God." This explains why the eternal theology also insists that a divine spark, soul, spirit, or Buddha-nature exists within us all. The eighteenth-century Rabbi Shmelke of Nikolsburg expressed this timeless conviction when he declared that "All souls are one. Each is a spark from the original soul, and this soul is wholly inherent in all souls." I have yet to meet a single person who has had a near-death experience or mystical experience who would disagree with this statement. As near-death experiencer Barbara Baird reminded me recently, "Nobody who has an out-of-body experience ever again questions whether or not they have a soul. They know they do." And most of them, like mystical experiencer Paul Palnik, are convinced that their souls are what bind them to God. "It became clear to me, without a question of doubt," he told me, "that within the innermost part of me, the innermost part of everyone, resides God." Or, as near-death experiencer Dr. Yvonne Kason stated earlier, "There is but one source, and we are all directly connected to that source."

The eternal theology insists that most people are sadly unaware of the fact that God resides within them, which explains why their lives are so often characterized by inner restlessness, discontent, and a profound sense of loneliness. It also explains why so many people are terribly selfish, deeply materialistic, and occasionally downright destructive. Having lost contact with the God within, the eternal theology says people lose the grace to see things as they truly are, to see things through the eyes of unity. As such, they become alienated from God and the flow of life in much the same way a newcomer occasionally feels alienated while standing alone at a party. While the newcomer may want to fully participate, he does not know how. He feels lost and left out.

The idea of being lost and left out is well expressed in the Christian concept of the Fall. It is also expressed through the Buddhist idea of *dukka,* or suffering, and in the Hindu notion of avidya, or ignorance. What we are ignorant of, say the eternal theologians, is our undeniable belonging to the source of all creation.

Since we are lost and estranged from God, we must find our way home. This is why the spiritual journey, if anything, is a journey home. The eternal theology says that we begin this journey by working to rediscover the divine spark that resides within, whether through prayer, meditation, contemplation, compassionate service, or the study of sacred scripture. But most of us find the divine spark when we are able to step beyond ourselves through the practice of love, because love provides the only truly accurate compass for the journey home. As Saint John the Evangelist wrote, "Love comes from God; and everyone who loves is begotten by God and knows God; those who don't love, don't know God; for God is love." If we are successful in this loving endeavor to connect with the Divine, whatever feelings of loneliness, or homesickness, we might have will vanish entirely because salvation, or enlightenment, is really nothing more than the realization of our attachment to the whole of God's creation.

The eighteenth-century spiritual visionary Rabbi Aaron of Karlin summed up the essence of this eternal theology as follows: "There is a divine light in every soul, it is dormant and eclipsed by the follies of this world. We must first awaken this light, then the upper light will come upon us. In Thy light which is within us will we see light." Those who undergo NDEs and mystical experiences obviously achieve this realization of light, however briefly. I believe this is why these experiences so often change people's lives so profoundly, and why they fill them with such immeasurable joy. They were lost, but now they are found. As mystical experiencer Dr. Alfred Painter told us earlier:

> I was swept away with an immense feeling of joy and belonging. . . . The walls that separated me from the world dissolved and a great weight was lifted from my shoulders. Sensing the surge of life in everything around me, I knew, for the first time in my life, that I really did belong to the world and that everything was as it should be.

The eternal theologians recognized that it is difficult to learn to love so long as we take ourselves, or our spiritual journeys, too seriously. This is why they so often stressed that it is actually a mistake to actively seek out spiritual experiences, mystical, near-death, or otherwise. The eternal theologians felt strongly that peak moments should occur naturally, by grace, because they understood that those who seek enlightenment or salvation too avidly often face the danger of becoming self-absorbed rather than self-forgetful. "If you would find yourself you must first lose yourself," is a universal maxim of spiritual life. I believe this explains why some variation of the concept of "the middle way" is found in nearly every religion. The Buddha defined the middle way as a path somewhere between hedonism (self-indulgence) and asceticism (self-denial). In his youth he had tried both paths, only to learn that when we seek anything too avidly, whether it be spiritual enlightenment or the highs of sex, we are then less likely to experience the true fruits of love, self-transcendence, and a rich experience of God. Those who hope to make the journey home must relax, in other words, for we cannot experience the delights of travel until we forget the destination, or, as the late singer Harry Chapin once put it in a popular song, "It's got to be the goin', not the getting there, that's good."

Learning to relax into the mystery of life is an important aim on the journey home. But so, too, is helping the man with the flat tire on the roadside. The eternal theology has always stressed that we grow in knowledge of God by performing virtuous acts, because, as Jesus told us, "The measure by which you give is the measure by which you will receive." When we give of ourselves to creation wholeheartedly we naturally overcome self-centeredness and increase our sense of belonging to God. Near-death experiencer Dr. George Rodonaia wonderfully expressed this perennial truth when he told us earlier that "Anyone who has had such an experience of God . . . knows that there is only one truly significant work to do in life, and that is to love—to love nature, to love people, to love animals, to love creation itself, just because it is. To serve God's creation with a warm and loving hand of generosity and compassion—that is the only meaningful existence."

While the eternal theology says that a good way to find God is through loving communities gathered in his name, inner spirituality is considered more important than institutional conformity. In the eternal theology, people do not need a mediator between themselves and God. The Buddha stressed this in his oft-quoted statement "Be a lamp to yourself." Or, as it is written in the Bible, "I have put truth in your innermost mind, and I have written it in your heart. No longer does a man need to teach his brother about God. For all of you know Me, from the most ignorant to the most learned, from the poorest to the most powerful." As mystical experiencer Claudia Michele earlier declared: "There is no human authority. None. No president or priest, counselor or doctor can provide us with what we are not ready to experience. . . . If anyone assumes they have the answers for you, they are a false messiah."

The eternal theology has seldom focused on the problem of evil, but rather on the problem of how to help people become more human. I believe this is why the eternal theologians generally said that only the Creator is in a position to judge creation. When it comes to judging others, humans do best to remain silent. Jesus expressed this sentiment well when he asserted, "Don't judge, and you will not be judged; don't condemn, and you will not be condemned; forgive, and you will be forgiven; give, and it will be given to you."

Finally, the eternal theology holds that those who are graced with a realization of their fundamental relatedness to God grow fully alive because, as Saint Irenaeus put it, "The glory of God is the human being fully alive." In other words, when we become fully alert and responsive to the many surprising gifts of everyday life, we are living spiritually.

In the end, the eternal theologians said that we cannot make the journey home if we are deep in sleep. We must first wake up to the gift of life. Perhaps this is why they repeatedly declared that what we believe, or claim to believe, is not terribly significant. What alone matters, they said, is what we do, how we live. It is for each of us to find the courage within ourselves to become truly good people, truly spiritual people, truly alive and vibrant and gracious and caring people. What it all comes down to, they insisted, is the subject of the following chapter—action, putting one's beliefs into practice amid the many stresses and strains of daily life. Fortunately, as the eternal theologian Goethe reminded us, "The moment one definitely commits oneself, then providence moves too. . . . Whatever you think you can do or believe you can do, begin it. Action has magic, grace, and power in it."

13

AT HOME IN THE HOUSE
OF LIFE

∞

All that matters is to be at one with the living God
to be a creature in the house of the God of life.

Like a cat asleep on a chair
at peace, in peace
and at one with the master of the house, with the mistress,
at home, at home in the house of the living,
sleeping on the hearth, and yawning before the fire.

Sleeping on the hearth of the living world
yawning at home before the fire of life
feeling the presence of the living God
like a great reassurance
a deep calm in the heart
a presence
as of the master sitting at the board
in his own house and greater being,
in the house of life.

—D. H. Lawrence

Several years ago, at the close of a worship service in the
Crown Heights section of New York, a young boy posed an
intriguing question to the late Lubavitcher Rebbe, spiritual

leader to the world's Lubavitcher Hasidic Jews. "Do Jews believe in the concept of reincarnation," he asked the aged, gray-bearded rabbi. "Of course we do," he replied. Then, with a wide smile growing on his face, he added, "But only a fool would wait to be reincarnated."

Wiser words have seldom been spoken. Only a fool would wait to be reincarnated, because the opportunity for rebirth exists anew each day; we can all wake up, over and over again, to the enduring mystery and beauty of life. Yet, "If you are in love, then why are you asleep?" wonders the poet Kabir. In essence, this is the great challenge, the great message I have taken from those who have had near-death experiences and mystical experiences: we need not die to experience spiritual fulfillment, we need only wake up to begin the journey home.

But what does "waking up" entail? And how is it accomplished in daily life? Fortunately, near-death experiencers and mystical experiencers have left us with a great many clues, the most important of which is that we must always strive to remember that the meaning of the word *religion* is to bind ourselves to that which is greater than we are. Therefore, anything that helps to bind us more intimately to life takes us closer to home, while anything that hampers this process leads us further astray. I believe this is why many of the people I interviewed for this book told me that for them religion was nothing more than training in the art of love, which is essentially about learning to live as selflessly as possible. As so many experiencers told me, "I lost myself in the loving oneness of the light."

So the goal of spiritual life is not to "get in touch with oneself," but to grow beyond oneself, to make room for the rediscovery of God, not only within, but without. While few near-death experiencers and mystical experiencers I met made any bold claims to great success in this effort, most told me they occasionally caught a glimmer of light in the midst of their daily rounds, and along with it the hope that they might one day fully awaken to joy in the sheer fact, the wondrous miracle, of life itself. In their efforts to achieve this spiritual awakening, the near-death experiencers and mystical experiencers I spoke with shared with me an abundance of useful lessons, one of which is the enormous importance of sustaining a lasting love affair with nature.

REVERENCE FOR LIFE

Each spring, in early April, I hose down my little rowing scull and cart it down to a river near my home. During the next seven months I will row this boat nearly every day. When I'm lucky, I get in an hour, sometimes even two. In this indulgence of leisure I find that my senses are rekindled, for here along the shores of Lake Erie, where I live, there are thousands of birds. When I row up river, into the secluded waters of a little lagoon I like to frequent, I see herons, ducks, bluebirds . . . an amazing diversity of life. Often, just sitting there in that little scull, I am transported to another world. While the city of Cleveland is just twelve miles away, I am alone in the magical world of nature, where I occasionally experience a special sense of intimacy with the diverse life that thrives along the river. Occasionally, I even feel my connection, however distant, to the birds and the water and the trees, all the way back to the stars, to the heavens, to the instant of creation itself. At such moments I am overcome with feelings of great peace and belonging, and a quiet stillness overcomes me. At the same time, however, I am also often filled with a heightened sense of responsibility, perhaps something akin to what the late Dr. Albert Schweitzer felt for the extraordinary abundance of life that surrounded his little makeshift hospital in the jungles of Equatorial Africa. When you love something, I've learned, responsibility quickly follows.

Although Dr. Schweitzer did not coin the famous phrase "reverence for life" until the 1950s, near-death experiencers and mystics have understood and practiced a similar reverence for life for many centuries. As a result of their recognition of the essential unity of life, their ethical system has always been grounded in the concept of the interconnectedness and mutual interdependency of all things. As many of the experiencers I spoke with told me, the gift of human existence entails tremendous responsibility for God's creation because we live in partnership with the universe; we belong to God just as surely as God belongs to us. Here is how Paul Palnik explained it to me:

> After feeling the oneness I experienced in my mystical moment I realized that I lived connected to all things, to birds, to trees, to other people, and a natural reverence for life just filled me; a reverence for the majesty of existence, the beauty of existence. Ever since then I dodge bugs on sidewalks, carry out spiders from my home. I just can't kill things I belong to. I find now that there is a sacredness to life, and I try to experience that sense of sacredness whenever I can by treating everyone, and everything, with the same respect I try to offer myself.

The concept of reverence for life described by Palnik has often been made out to be terribly complicated by academic philosophers, but I really can't see why. For those who truly revere God's creation, it quickly becomes obvious that anything that preserves and enhances life is essentially good, while anything that destroys, diminishes, or demeans life is bad. Reverence for life is simply about striving to widen the "circle of our compassion" to encompass all living creatures, all nature, all life. No one has stated this noble truth, this great spiritual necessity, with more clarity than Albert Einstein:

> A human being is part of the whole, called by us the "Universe," a part limited in time and space. He experiences himself, his thoughts and feelings, as something separate from the rest—a kind of optical delusion of his consciousness. This decision is a kind of prison for us, restricting us to our personal desires and to affection for a few persons nearest to us. Our task must be to free ourselves from this prison by widening our circle of compassion to embrace all living creatures and the whole of nature in its beauty.

SACRED DEEDS

Loving, compassionate service to others comes naturally to those who revere life, because it is through love that we experience not only the ties that bind us deeply to the God within, but which bind us to the God outside. Albert Schweitzer explained the practical benefits of this outlook when he wrote that "Whenever my life devotes itself in any way to life, my finite will-to-live experiences union with the infinite will in which all life is one, and I enjoy a feeling of refreshment which prevents me from pining away in the desert of life."

In my own tradition of Judaism, reverence for life is often expressed through the sacred deeds we call "mitzvahs." The word literally means "commandments," and it is understood to mean that all of us are commanded to do good deeds—not because they may bring us fame or attention, or win us abundant credits in a heavenly ledger, but because we lose ourselves in the process of heartfelt giving.

Sacred deeds are an excellent way to lose ourselves, and in my experience there is never any shortage of opportunities to perform them. Martin Buber once made this point wonderfully when he said that the world is not divided between the sacred and the profane, but between the holy and the not-yet-holy. All that is ever really needed for something to become holy, he said, is for a person to step in and realize its potential for holiness. Caring for a lonely senior, feeding the homeless, sending clothing and supplies for disaster relief—these are all mitzvahs that help make life holier.

In my own life, I have found that the best way to perform mitzvahs is in a spirit of togetherness, as though I were walking with God, which is the oldest form of piety expressed in the Bible: "It has been told thee, O man, what is good, and what the Lord doth require of thee: only to do justly, to love mercy and to walk humbly with thy God."

Learning how to do justly, love mercy, and walk humbly with God has long been considered one of the primary goals of spiritual life, but we all know from experience how very difficult this is. Humility, for one thing, does not come easy for any of us. It may well be the rarest virtue of our time. But this should not deter us from giving to others. As near-death experiencer Barbara Baird reminded me, "being spiritually perfect is not a prerequisite for giving." In other words, we need not all be mothers of charity, like Mother Teresa of Calcutta, to care for others. The act of giving a toy to a poor child, for example, is valuable regardless of whether or not we perform the deed in a state of perfect sentiment. The deed alone is what is most important because good deeds have a way of igniting genuine feelings of love somewhere along the line. The Christian concept of "agape," the practice of loving the unlovable, justifies "going through the motions" on these grounds, because spirituality is the goal, not the way of human beings. Only through the at-

186

tempt, in other words, the aspiration to become more loving, can one grow to see the world through sacred eyes. As mystical experiencer Claudia Michele explained to me:

> I have found that the more I nurture the ground around me, the more I nurture my own soul. And the more I nurture my own soul, the more I nurture the ground around me. So I've never viewed giving to others as a hardship, but as a blessing, because giving expands my soul. I believe that giving genuinely to others enhances the likelihood of healthy living, which is just another way of saying a spiritually full life. As I like to say, when the tree blooms, it is self-actualizing, and when we live in a healthy way, we are also self-actualizing. So the investment in helping others is also an investment in yourself.

GRATITUDE

Each night before dinner, we say a prayer at our table. Our little prayers are informal and occasionally downright funny, but they always tend to focus on the things we are grateful for. My little son often says a few words about how much he enjoyed playing with his friends at school that day. More often than not, my wife says a few things about how happy she is that we are all together as a family. And I often talk about the surprising or beautiful things I either saw or experienced that day.

Our family prayers, though seldom very eloquent, have become an important ritual in our family, particularly since the death of our daughter, because she taught us so much about the blessing of life. We have so much to be thankful for. Unfortunately, many of us fail to recognize this until very late in our lives, or until we are hit with a painful disease or a life-threatening illness. In my research on the spiritual dimensions of late life, for example, I was often struck by how many elderly people told me, in one way or another, that as time diminishes, its preciousness increases— that the closer they got to the end of their lives, the more they came to appreciate them. Dr. John Schneeweis, Jr., a Minnesota man I interviewed who was suffering from a glandular cancer of unknown origin, captured this truth eloquently just a few months before he passed away. "There are many days that the sense of life that I have is heightened beyond any other period in my life," he told me. "The awareness of being alive, and being conscious of what a treasure that is . . . for all its suffering and tragedy, it still is wonderful. In fact, sometimes, when I'm in public, it takes everything I have to keep from just whooping out loud at the wonderfulness of being alive."[1]

"Whooping out loud at the wonderfulness of being alive"—what a magnificent expression! This is certainly one of the great goals of spiritual life, and experience has taught me that a good way to get there is to begin by cultivating simple gratitude. As mystical experiencer Dr. Alfred Painter shared with me, "Saying thank you is more than good manners—it is good spirituality."

THE WILL TO WONDER

Unlike many people today who believe that everything will eventually be explained by science, most near-death experiencers and mystical experiencers I met were filled with a rich sense of surprise and wonder at the beauty and magnificence of life. Their religious experiences convinced them that they belonged to something far more mysterious than they could ever hope to fully comprehend, let alone describe. They developed not only the will to believe, you might say, but the will to wonder. I think this is why so many of them told me that they found life a great deal more surprising and spectacular after their spiritual experiences. "Suddenly upon my return," said one near-death experiencer, "the world looked new and beautiful."

For those who view life in such a state of wonder, boredom is nearly impossible, ingratitude unthinkable. As Rabbi Abraham Joshua Heschel once explained, "The surest way to suppress our ability to understand the meaning of God ... is to take things for granted. Indifference to the sublime wonder of living is the root of sin. The way to faith leads through acts of wonder and radical amazement." Sunsets, good food and wine, warm conversation, the birth of a child, the pleasures of touch, the blessings of natural beauty—are these not all surprising and wonderful gifts freely given to us by the grace of God? A ninety-two-year-old woman once summed up this pro-wonder, pro-gratitude attitude nicely when she told me that

> I have finally learned to open my eyes and give in to the puzzle of what's around me. I've given up thinking I will ever be able to understand or explain everything, because it takes a lot of the joy out of living. I wish it didn't take me so long to see this. Now I try hard not to complain about life, or the nagging little pains of old age, because I see that life is a privilege denied to many. So long as I keep this in mind, I find it hard not to look at each new day as anything but a surprising gift from God. . . . Each day that I live is a gift of grace.

HOSPITALITY

For those who are open to life's many mysteries, hospitality comes naturally. Coffee is always brewing, the teapot ever boiling, because one never knows when an opportunity to connect with another person is at hand. Who knows when we will hear the sound of the door being knocked upon? Best be prepared. I believe this is why truly spiritual people are in the habit of cultivating the nearly forgotten art of basic hospitality, perhaps because they realize that when we are able to make others feel comfortable, the pleasures of belonging are close at hand.

In my work with near-death experiencers and mystical experiencers, I was nearly always treated kindly and with openness. As I've learned, for those who feel at home in life, hostility is an alien attitude. Fear of differences is, too, I've noted. I believe this is why so many of the people I interviewed were genuinely curious about me and what I had to say. More than a few of them were anxious to turn the tables on me. "Now, what do *you* believe?" they often asked.

Those who feel good about life, good about themselves, are confident enough to live with open doors, open arms. They seek to find and emphasize those beliefs that bind them to others rather than the ones that tear them apart. This is why racism, classism, and bigotry are always foreign traits to spiritually minded people. Hatred, after all, is the utter antithesis of hospitality, insofar as those who hate are in the business of snapping connections, not forging them.

Hospitable people are also good listeners, which explains why listening has long been considered one of the most important habits to cultivate if we wish to get closer to God. In my own life I've found that when I am able to listen carefully enough to anyone, listen to them with my full heart, then the walls of separation come crumbling down. Martin Buber believed that such "active listening" is not only the secret to fulfilling relationships between people, but a vital passageway to faith. Near-death experiencer Barbara Baird agrees, because she is convinced that

Listening is holy. Every time I sit down to talk with another person, I know that if I listen carefully enough, I can make a difference in their lives. And if I can make a difference in their lives, it will surely make a difference in mine. Listening expands my soul.

One thing that has become very clear to me is that it is impossible to truly help people unless we really care to hear what they are saying. If we are unwilling to cultivate a listening ear, we cannot speak a language that will heal. That's why I so often pray: God, please help me listen carefully enough so I can make a positive difference in people's lives.

COMMUNITY

More and more, the concept of community is dying in our time, succumbing to the ever-increasing demands of what sociologist of religion Dr. Robert Bellah has called "rampant individualism." In my view, this is terribly unfortunate, because the core of the word *community* is "to commune," or to connect with others in a significant way. My wife, Anne, cares deeply about this subject, because she believes quite strongly, as she recently wrote, "that one of the great blessings of life is to find a community of people who support one another in their common quest for meaning. . . . One of the most overlooked benefits of finding such a supportive community is that through the sharing of the chores of life (from child care to meal preparation to supportive conversation) community members suddenly find themselves with more time to truly live, to truly celebrate the gift of life."

Developing such a spirit of community doesn't come easy in our time. Not because we don't have enough religion, I'm afraid, but because we do not have enough spirituality. In my travels throughout America, one of the most dismaying things I noticed is that our religious communities drive us apart more often than they bring us together. All too frequently, we use our religion as a tool to distinguish ourselves from one another, at the expense of developing a wider feeling of community. Mystical experiencer Dr. Alfred Painter, a former Methodist minister, felt quite strongly that this was the wrong approach to creating community:

> I learned as a minister that many people come to church for social reasons, not spiritual ones. They often come to set themselves apart from others, not to stand in concert with them. This is a sort of Band-Aid for the soul that usually does more harm than good. In the short term, it provides people with a sense of community and a specific identity, but in the long run it only estranges them from a wider participation in life.... It cuts people off from God instead of bringing them closer to God.
>
> If there is an answer to this problem, I think it is found in just getting people talking, thinking, and sharing, because sooner or later they will come to realize that there is more to life than they could ever possibly hope to understand. This humbles them a bit, as I suppose it should, but it also deepens their understanding of how dependent they are on others, on all of creation, on God. Get people talking like this, and pretty soon they get honest with each other, and from that point on the spirit of true community begins to emerge. They begin to see that they don't function in an arbitrary or independent manner, but are actually connected to all things, which in my view is the basis for all true community, all spiritual growth.

THE HAPPINESS OF PURSUIT

A question that has long engaged me is why so many people never seem to find lasting happiness. Never before in history have we had so much freedom to pursue happiness, and never before have we had so much materially—so why is it that so many of us are so miserable?

The answer, I've come to believe, is that happiness just can't be pursued. Rather, like the profound spiritual experiences that graced the lives of those I have profiled in this book, happiness must emerge naturally as we throw ourselves into the task of living. Dr. Viktor Frankl came to much the same conclusion when he cautioned us never to "aim at success—the more you aim at it and make it a target, the more you are going to miss it. For success, like happiness, cannot be pursued; it must ensue . . . as the unintended side-effect of one's personal dedication to a course greater than oneself."

Frankl sheds light on why so many of the people I interviewed were not much interested in the pursuit of happiness but rather in the happiness of pursuit. They came to conclude, as did mystical experiencer Linda Richard, that the great challenge of spiritual life is not to vigorously seek after pleasure, but to enter more deeply into the present, all day long:

> To laugh, to frolic, to take my shoes off and walk in the sand by the waterside—these, to me, are the stuff of life. If another mystical experience should come upon me, that would be fine. But I don't need this to know that God resides in all things, is present in all things. I don't need to chase after what is right in front of me anymore, do I? The spiritual life isn't about chasing after anything. It's about waking up to everything. What could be simpler than that?

Yes, I know. This is a simple lesson, but it is true: if we can find God through the happiness that ensues from our daily pursuits, through the little things we not only must do, but choose to do, we will soon find that the journey home is not a journey at all, but rather the rediscovery of what we knew all along; that home is wherever we happen to be when we wake up to the miracle of the present. Again, as Kabir asks, "If you are in love, then why are you asleep?"

Maybe the old railroad crossing signs said it even better: STOP, LOOK, AND LISTEN.

THE DISTANT VIEW

∞

We must all become familiar with the thought of death if we want to grow into really good people. We need not think of it every day or every hour. But when the path of life leads us to some vantage point where the scene around us fades away and we contemplate the distant view right to the end, let us not close our eyes. Let us pause for a moment, look at the distant view, and then carry on.

Thinking about death in this way produces true love for life. When we are familiar with death, we accept each week, each day, as a gift. Only if we are able thus to accept life—bit by bit—does it become precious.

—Albert Schweitzer

During the time it has taken me to complete this book, several people I have known and cared about have died. A former professor and dear friend, Dr. Wilbur Friddell, made the decision to end his daily dialysis treatments in August of 1994 and passed away peacefully a week later at his home in Santa Barbara. One of my hospice patients here in Cleveland finally let go, in November of 1994, after a long and painful bout with lung cancer. A thirty-seven year-old lawyer who represented my family died from a brain tumor in February of 1995. And the playwright Robert E. Lee, who supported me graciously in my early career, also recently passed away, in California, at the age of seventy-six.

While attending a memorial service for my most recent hospice patient to die, I had plenty of time to reflect upon my friends, my life, this book. As I sat there, amid the many weeping friends of the deceased, and with a few tears of my own, it occurred to me that funerals serve a terribly important function in our society, because death is a potent wake-up call for the living to get up and live. This is why I believe God may well have good reasons for keeping the ultimate mystery of death a secret from most of us, because it is only when we reflect upon our deaths that we can fully fathom how genuinely precious our lives really are.

As for me, I am striving now to become more comfortable with all that I don't know; I am working hard, as I often tell my wife, to truly let go into the mystery of life, because I find that when I do, love comes more easily to me. What matters to me more than anything else these days is to live in an affectionate universe, not only because I believe affection is the only real basis for authentic spiritual life, but because the older I get the more I see that the men and women I interviewed for this book are right: death holds little fear for those who have learned to love. Perhaps the sculptor Ivan Mestrovic captured this eternal truth even better in the following words he engraved on a cathedral bell: "Learn the secret of love, and you will discover the secret of Death—and belief in Life Eternal."

In the meantime, like most of us, I stumble along, occasionally doing very stupid things in my efforts to learn the secret of love. But I've learned to forgive myself for the majority of these silly missteps, and I find that when I do, I often experience a beautiful richness of life; feelings of great joy overcome me, just because I am alive and here and able to see, touch, taste, and smell. What a marvelous miracle to be alive! On occasion, I even feel so good, so deeply connected to life, so at home in it all, that I believe, deep down in my heart, that mystical experiencer Robert Cubin was right: "Death, that great puzzle, is no longer a mystery.... It is the most wonderful, joyous, sensitive, journey home."

NOTES

Chapter 3
1. R. Noyes, Jr. "The Experience of Dying," *Psychiatry*, 1972 (35) 174–84.
2. Raymond Moody. *Life After Life* (New York: Bantam, 1976), pp. 21–23.

Chapter 4
1. Melvin Moorse. *Closer to the Light* (New York: Ivy, 1990), p. 35.

Chapter 6
1. L. Morabito. "Love and God in the Near-Death Experience," *Journal of Near Death Studies*, 1990 (97) 65–66.
2. Kenneth Ring. *Heading Toward Omega* (New York: William Morrow, 1989), p. 62.
3. K. Ring and S. Franklin. "Do Suicide Survivors Report Near Death Experiences?" *Omega*, 1991 (12) 191–208.
4. Margo Grey. *Return from Death* (London: Arkana, 1985), p. 48.
5. David N. Bell. "The Vision of the World and of the Arche-

types in the Latin Spirituality of the Middle Ages," *Archives d'histoire doctrinale et Litteraire du Moyen Age,* 1977 (44) 7–31.

Chapter 7

1. Raymond Moody. *Reflections on Life After Life* (Covington, GA: Mockingbird Books, 1977).
2. R.W. Emerson. *Complete Works* (London: Routledge, 1897), p. 59.
3. P.M.H. Atwater. *Coming Back to Life* (New York: Ballantine, 1988), p. 38.
4. Kenneth Ring. *Heading Toward Omega* (New York: William Morrow, 1989), p. 67.

Chapter 8

1. Kenneth Ring. *Heading Toward Omega* (New York: William Morrow, 1989). p. 69.
2. C. Sutherland. "Changes in Religious Beliefs, Attitudes, and Practices Following Near-Death Experiences: An Australian Study," *Journal of Near-Death Studies,* 1990 (9) 21–31.
3. Raymond Moody. *The Light Beyond* (New York: Bantam Books, 1988), p. 42.
4. Kenneth Ring. *Heading Toward Omega,* p. 70.
5. M. Insinger. "The Impact of a Near-Death Experience on Family Relationships," *Journal of Near-Death Studies,* 1991 (9) 141–181.
6. Margot Grey. *Return from Death* (London: Arkana, 1985), p. 27.

Chapter 9

1. Phillip L. Berman, ed. *The Courage of Conviction* (New York: Dodd, Mead, 1985), p. 75.

Chapter 11
1. Ralph W. Hood. "Personality Correlates of the Report of Mystical Experience," *Psychological Reports,* 1979 (44.3) 804–6.

Chapter 13
1. Phillip L. Berman. *The Search for Meaning* (New York: Ballantine, 1990), p. 447.

BIBLIOGRAPHY

Sources on Near-Death Experiences

Atwater, P.M.H. *Coming Back to Life* (New York: Ballantine, 1988).

Barrett, William F. *Deathbed Visions* (London: n.p., 1926).

Berman, Alan L. "Belief in Afterlife, Religion, Religiosity and Life-Threatening Experiences, *Omega: Journal of Death and Dying* 5 (1974).

Doore, Gary. *What Survives? Contemporary Explorations of Life After Death* (Los Angeles: Tarcher, 1990).

Eastman, Margaret. "The Evidence for Out-of-Body Experiences," *Proceedings, Society for Psychical Research* 53 (December 1962).

Gallup, George, Jr., with William Proctor. *Adventures in Immortality: A Look Beyond the Threshold of Death.* (New York: McGraw Hill, 1982).

Greyson, Bruce, and Ian Stevenson. "The Phenomenology of Near-Death Experiences," *American Journal of Psychiatry* 137:10 (October 1980).

Greyson, Bruce, and N.E. Bush. *Psychiatry* 55:95–109 (1992).

Heim, Albert. "Notizen uber den Tod durch Absturz," *Jahrbuch des schweizer Alpen Club* 27 (1892). [Translated by Noyes and

Kletti, "The Experience of Dying from Falls," *Omega: Journal of Death & Dying*, Volume 3, 1972.]

Hyslop, James H. "Visions of the Dying," *Journal of the American Society for Psychical Research* 1 (1907).

Kübler-Ross, Elisabeth. *Death: The Final Stage of Growth* (Englewood Cliffs, N.J.: n.p., 1975).

Lorimer, David. *Whole in One* (London: Arkana, 1990).

Moody, Raymond. *Life after Life* (New York: Bantam, 1976).

———. *The Light Beyond* (New York: Bantam, 1988).

———. *Reflections on Life After Life* (Covington, GA: Mockingbird Books, 1977).

Moorse, Melvin. *Closer to the Light* (New York: Ivy, 1990).

Myers, F.W.H. *Human Personality and Its Survival of Bodily Death* 2 vols. (New York: n.p., 1903).

Noyes, Russell, Jr. "The Art of Dying," *Perspectives in Biology and Medicine* (Spring, 1971).

———. "Attitude Change Following Near-Death Experiences," *Psychiatry* 43 (August 1980).

———. "Dying and Mystical Consciousness," *Journal of Thanatology* (January 1971).

Osis, Karlis. *Deathbed Observations by Physicians and Nurses. Parapsychological Monographs* (New York: n.p., 1961).

Rawlings, Maurice. *Beyond Death's Door* (Nashville: Thomas Nelson, 1978).

Ring, Kenneth. *Heading Toward Omega* (New York: William Morrow, 1989).

———. *Life at Death* (New York: Quill, 1980).

Ritchie, George G., Jr. *Return from Tomorrow* (Waco, Texas: Chosen Books, 1978).

Sabom, Michael B. *Recollections of Death: A Medical Investigation* (New York: Harper & Row, 1982).

Tart, Charles. "States of Consciousness and State-Specific Sciences," *Science* 176 (June 1972).

Vincent, Ken R. *Visions of God from the Near-Death Experience* (Burdett, N.Y.: Larson Publications, 1994).

Zaleski, Carol. *Otherworld Visions* (Oxford: Oxford University Press, 1987).

Sources on Mysticism, Religion, and Spirituality

Bridges, Hal. *American Mysticism* (Lakemont, Georgia: CSA Press, 1970).

Buber, Martin. *I and Thou*, trans. Walter Kaufmann (New York: Scribners, 1970).

———. *Eclipse of God* (New York: Harper, 1952).

Capra, Fritjof and David Stendl-Rast. *Belonging to the Universe* (New York: Harper Collins, 1991).

Conze, Edward. *Buddhist Wisdom Books* (London: Allen & Unwin, 1958).

Dosey, Larry. *Recovering the Soul* (New York: Bantam, 1989).

Einstein, Albert. *Ideas and Opinions*, reprinted. (New York: Dell, 1973).

Eliade, Mircea. *Patterns in Comparative Religion* (New York: Sheed & Ward, 1958).

Emerson, Ralph Waldo. *Complete Works* (London: Routledge, 1897).

Frankl, Viktor E. *Man's Search for Meaning* (New York: Simon & Schuster, 1959).

Heschel, Abraham Joshua. *God in Search of Man* (New York: Farrar, Straus, and Giroux, 1955).

———. *The Sabbath* (New York: Farrar, Straus, and Giroux, 1951).

Huxley, Aldous. *The Perennial Philosophy* (New York: Harper, 1944).

James, William. *The Varieties of Religious Experience. The Gifford Lectures on Natural Religion, Edinburgh, 1901–1902* (Cambridge, Mass., and London: 1985).

205

Jung, Carl G. *Memories, Dreams, Reflections,* ed. Aniela Jaffe; trans. Richard Winston and Clara Winston (New York: Vintage Books, 1965).

Kaltenmark, Max. *Lao Tzu and Taoism* (Stanford, Cal.: Stanford University Press, 1965).

Keating, Thomas. *Awakenings* (New York: Crossroad, 1991).

Kushner, Harold. *Who Needs God* (New York: Summit Books, 1989).

Maslow, Abraham. *Motivation and Personality* (New York: Harper & Row, 1954).

———. *Religion, Values and Peak Experiences* (New York: Viking, 1964).

———. *The Farther Reaches of Human Nature* (New York: Viking, 1971).

Mitchell, Stephen. *The Enlightened Heart* (New York: Harper Collins, 1989).

———. *The Enlightened Mind* (New York: Harper Collins, 1991).

Moore, Thomas. *Care of the Soul* (New York: Harper Collins, 1993).

Nouwen, Henri J.M. *Reaching Out: The Three Movements of Spiritual Life* (New York: Doubleday, 1986).

Rinpoche, Sogyal. *The Tibetan Book of Living and Dying* (San Francisco: Harper Collins, 1993).

Schweitzer, Albert. *Reverence for Life* (New York: Harper & Row, 1966).

———. *Out of My Life and Thought* (New York: Holt, Rinehart & Winston, 1933).

———. *The Mysticism of Paul the Apostle* (London: Allen & Unwin, 1931).

Smith, Huston. *Forgotten Truth* (New York: Harper, 1976).

———. *Beyond the Post-Modern Mind* (Wheaton, Illinois: Quest Books, 1982).

Steindl-Rast, David. *A Listening Heart* (New York: Crossroad, 1992).

————. *Gratefulness, the Heart of Prayer* (New York: Paulist Press, 1984).

Swedenborg, Emanuel. *Heaven and Hell* (London: Swendenborg Society, 1958).

Underhill, Evelyn. *Practical Mysticism,* reprint ed. (Columbus, Ohio: Ariel Press, 1987).

————. *Mysticism,* reprint ed. (New York: Doubleday, 1990).

ABOUT THE AUTHOR

Phillip L. Berman, who was educated in philosophy and religion at the University of California and at Harvard, is the author of *The Courage of Conviction*, nominated for the Kennedy Book Award, and *The Search for Meaning*, nominated for the Grawemeyer Award in Religion. He is also past president of the Center for the Study of Contemporary Belief, and winner of the Lillich Davidson Book Award. A member of the American Academy of Religion, he is a leading lecturer in the United States on spiritual values and lifelong development. He also produces special reports on religion for ABC TV (WEWS news) in Cleveland. He makes his home in Lakewood, Ohio, with his wife, the author and journalist Anne Gordon, and their six-year-old son, Aaron.